7 STEPS FOR SUCCESS

HIGH SCHOOL TO COLLEGE TRANSITION
STRATEGIES FOR STUDENTS WITH DISABILITIES

Council for
Exceptional
Children

ELIZABETH C. HAMBLET

ISBN 0-86586-467-5

Copyright © 2011 by the Council for Exceptional Children, 2900 Crystal Drive, Suite 1000, Arlington, VA 22202-3557

Stock No. P6041

Graphic Design and Layout: Carol L. Williams

Printed in the United States of America.

10 9 8 7 6 5 4 3 2 1

Dedication

For Eric, Olivia, and Evan, and Mom and Dad.

How privileged I am to have a wonderful family

with whom I can share my life.

And for Allison—the best student I know.

Table of Contents

Foreword by Loring C. Brinckerhoff . . . . *vii*

Acknowledgments. . . . . *ix*

Preface . . . . *xi*

*Step 1   Establish a Foundation: Learn About the Law and
          the Research on Preparing for Success at College* *1*

Step 2   Know Student Rights and Responsibilities *15*

Step 3   Develop Essential Personal Skills *29*

Step 4   Develop College Survival Skills *51*

Step 5   Understand College Accommodations *71*

Step 6   Find the Right College. *97*

*Step 7   Put It All Together: Documentation and the
          Transition Portfolio* *127*

Epilogue: The College Experience. *147*

References. *157*

Foreword

Elizabeth Hamblet is an experienced special educator who has taken a broad look at the sometimes complicated postsecondary landscape and described it in a manner that is understandable to parents, professionals, and students alike.

This practical guide describes the rights and responsibilities that students with disabilities have as they transition from high school to college. As Ms. Hamblet reminds readers, colleges and universities are not required to modify their curriculum or lower admission standards for students with disabilities. Students with disabilities must meet the same criteria for entrance to college or programs and maintain the same GPA as their peers without disabilities.

This guide provides a wealth of insight into the complexities of the college search process for prospective students and their families. By employing the voices of seasoned guidance counselors, admissions directors, disability coordinators, and students with disabilities, it addresses some of the most commonly asked questions in regards to disability disclosure, the admissions essay, test score interpretation, and what "works" for students at college. It also includes practical suggestions regarding how to make the most of the campus visit and questions to ask the disability services coordinator.

Ms. Hamblet speaks directly to young adults with disabilities about the types of disability documentation they need to provide, how to ask for accommodations, and most important, how to advocate for themselves with college faculty. Students who learn how to articulate their disability in plain language, demonstrate their self-knowledge, and know how to utilize available campus resources, such as the Disability Services office, the counseling center, learning center, and writing lab are more likely to achieve greater success in college than students who elect to hide their disability and go it alone.

The transition from high school is always challenging for high school students, but for young adults with disabilities it can be even more difficult. However, this process of self-discovery can be enhanced with self-advocacy and a solid foundation of the disability laws, postsecondary options, and the range of support services available to students with disabilities in higher education. It's a new era, and the possibilities are limitless—both in the classroom and online.

Loring C. Brinckerhoff, Ph.D.

Acknowledgments

I would like to express my deepest gratitude to the Council for Exceptional Children for making this project a reality. How lucky I am that CEC Director of Publications, Stefani Roth, shared my vision; her enthusiasm paved the way for a project that I had for so long hoped to bring to fruition. CEC's support will help me to reach so many more students than I could ever hope to reach on my own. And in extending that reach, I would like to thank—effusively—Lorraine Sobson, who deserves the credit for transforming this from a dry, linear instruction manual into an approachable, digestible guide for all audiences.

My thanks go out to the college and high school professionals who offered their advice and instructive tales. Their insights provide such valuable, practical information for students, and for the parents and professionals whose goal it is to help them make a successful transition.

The students who contributed to this book deserve tremendous praise for their willingness to share their stories. Through their candor, they have offered a mix of reality-check and hope that is everything an author could hope to pass on. Their contributions provide students with a balanced view of life at college and offer proof that earning a college degree is a very achievable goal. I am truly grateful to them for their willingness and eagerness to share their experiences so that other students might benefit.

I would remiss if I did not thank Loring Brinckerhoff, my mentor over a number of years and geographical regions. He is both a role model and a dear friend, and his tutelage has been invaluable.

Preface

The world has changed tremendously for students with disabilities over the past several decades. Laws have been put in place to make college more accessible, and the public's understanding of students with disabilities has evolved. These students are graduating from the most competitive institutions in the country with the highest degrees and going on to fulfilling careers. This is great news!

Yet some students with disabilities experience a really difficult transition to college. Although most students—with and without disabilities—struggle to adjust to the college environment, students with disabilities also have to deal with changes in the support system—both in their responsibilities and in the level of support available. So much of their distress could be avoided if students gain a better understanding of the college environment while they are in high school, so that they can prepare for it.

Steps 1 and 2 lay out a legal foundation for readers. It is crucial for students to understand what the law says about disability services at college so that they can be clear about their rights and responsibilities. Steps 3 and 4 discuss the self-management and academic skills that have been shown by research to be linked with success at college, so that parents, professionals and students can make sure that students' high school years are spent developing these important strategies. Step 5 reviews accommodations that are and are not frequently available so that students' Individualized education programs and 504 plans reflect the goal of working toward their independence in academic and personal functioning by the time they finish high school. Step 6 offers answers to frequently asked questions about admissions from seasoned counselors. They discuss choosing a college and offer their thoughts on how much students should disclose about their disability during the application process. Step 7 provides guidance to make sure that students have the necessary paperwork to apply for accommodations at college and offers ideas for developing a transition portfolio to help in the collection of information to aid students' transition. And, finally, the epilogue shares the experiences and reflections of students with disabilities who have already entered (and—in some cases—successfully exited) the college environment, in order to give students a real-life view of what the college environment might be like for them.

By giving students the proper preparation for college, we empower them to pursue success— not just at college, but after graduation, too. Although some of the items discussed in this book are specific to the college environment, the skills and self-knowledge that students are encouraged to develop will serve them well in their career and adult life, as well.

Step 1

Establish a Foundation:

Learn About the Law and the Research on Preparing for Success at College

Antidiscrimination laws created in the later part of the 20th century help make college an appropriate and accessible option for students with disabilities. Yet even though the first of these laws was passed over 30 years ago, many of these students, their families, and the high school professionals with whom they work often are unaware of the way that systems for supporting students with disabilities "work" at college. Depending upon the level of support students utilize, the differences between the high school and college environments can be considerable when it comes to disability services. In addition to understanding the changes in support services, it is also helpful to know a bit about the research on the college experience for students with disabilities and its implications for making the transition from high school.

Step 1

Establish a Foundation:

Learn About the Law and the Research on Preparing for Success at College

Throughout students' elementary and secondary education, most special education services are provided via individualized education programs (IEPs) under the Individuals With Disabilities Education Act (IDEA), so students are likely to have become accustomed to the supports and procedures that are part of this system of accommodation and instruction (Madaus, 2005). As students move from high school to college, there is a shift in the laws covering services for students with disabilities. Although some things, such as basic accommodations, may be similar for students, there are changes in the way the disability services system works at college; for some students, there may be a significant change in the supports available to them (Shaw, 2009).

Moving From IDEA to Section 504 and the Americans With Disabilities Act (ADA)—Changing Laws, Changing Service Models

While students are in high school, preparation for college typically focuses on selecting classes and participating in extracurricular activities to build a "college résumé." For students with disabilities, preparation for college should include an overview of how disability services and accommodations can differ so that students are prepared for these changes.

The reason that this kind of preparation is often missing from students' programming is that high school professionals themselves may be unaware of the changes. Special education teachers' training and work center on IDEA, which applies only in the K-to-12 system. Unless they have investigated the differences in college support services on their own, late elementary and secondary professionals are unlikely to know about how these differ, and therefore are unable to provide such information to families. Middle and high school special education professionals need to spend time familiarizing themselves with the services and accommodations available at college and with how students get access to them (Kochhar-Bryant, 2009) so they can help to educate families and provide a guiding hand in class placement and support decisions for students (see box, "The Professional Connection" on page 3; Shaw, 2009).

Some students with disabilities and their families are knowledgeable about the laws in effect at college and have expectations that align with typically available services, but many others are unaware that there are changes in the system at college. Some families think that the disability services model is the same as it is at high school, and they assume that colleges have to provide any accommodation contained in a student's **IEP** or **Section 504 Plan**. Others take a more dim view, assuming that there are no services available for students with disabilities at the college level. It helps students and their families to have information regarding changes at the college level—the existence of accommodations, as well as procedures and limitations—as early as the eighth grade, and certainly no later than when students are in the ninth grade (Banerjee & Brinckerhoff, 2009; Madaus, 2009).

The Individuals With Disabilities Education Act

High school special education services are governed by IDEA, the federal education law that requires schools in the public elementary and secondary system to identify students with disabilities and provide them with programs, specialized instruction, and other services via an IEP (Madaus & Shaw, 2004; McGuire, 2009). But IDEA only applies to the K-to-12 system (McGuire, 2009), so when students graduate their IEPs "expire." Because colleges are not covered by IDEA, they are not required to provide any of the services or adjustments outlined in students' IEPs. This doesn't mean that colleges will not offer students the same **accommodation** in their expired IEPs; indeed, colleges may offer students exactly the same adjustments they received in high school—or even some that students had not previously considered (see Step 5 for more on college accommodations). But the **disability services (DS) office** decides what type of services students will receive on the basis of whether those accommodations respond to the student's area of need, are available at the college, and are considered appropriate in the college environment. Students and their parents need to know that although colleges may choose to provide the same supports that students received in high school, they are not legally obligated to do so.

Section 504 and the Americans With Disabilities Act

Families should not fear the shift from IDEA to other laws when students move to college. Services are available at college and can be very supportive; they just work differently. The laws that provide for accommodations and services at college are Section 504 of the Rehabilitation Act of 1973 and the Americans With Disabilities Act (ADA;

The Professional Connection

High school child-study team professionals and outside therapists, psychologists, and social workers who work with students with disabilities should take an interest in educating themselves about the changes in the college environment. The HEATH Resource Center at the National Youth Transitions Center offers a downloadable "toolkit" that covers the law, documentation, accommodations, and other relevant topics at:

www.heath.gwu.edu/assets/33/toolkit.pdf

McGuire, 2009). The ADA was passed in 1990 to reinforce and expand Section 504; the ADA Amendments Act of 2008 (ADAAA) extended this protection to more individuals (Battle, 2004; McGuire, 2009).

Section 504 is a federal antidiscrimination law that requires schools from preschool through graduate school to avoid discrimination against students with disabilities by providing modifications and accommodations (Madaus, 2005). However, different sections of 504 apply to high schools and colleges (Subparts D and E, respectively), and each places different obligations on schools (McGuire, 2009). Like IEPS, 504 plans also "expire" when students graduate: Just as a high school student's IEP does not transfer to the college setting, neither does a student's existing 504 plan (Madaus, 2005).

Section 504 and the ADA are civil rights laws, not education laws; they cover education because it is a public service. Both laws are intended to prevent discrimination (McGuire, 2009). They mandate that colleges remove barriers that may prevent students with disabilities from accessing their services (e.g., dorms, classes, recreational facilities), and they guarantee students with disabilities certain rights at college. Even though these rights are not written explicitly into the laws' text, they are widely understood (see Step 2 for more on students' rights).

Supporting Students With Disabilities at the College Level

Providing a Level Playing Field

Section 504 and the ADA allow colleges certain rights with regard to deciding how to provide students with access to the curriculum (see box, "College Support Services at a Glance" on page 5). When granting accommodations, colleges are only required to "level the playing field," not to help students with disabilities achieve the same grades as their peers (Madaus & Shaw, 2004; McGuire, 2009). They are not required

---

Definitions

A Section 504 Plan details educational accommodations and modifications, generally covering students with disabilities who do not qualify for services under IDEA (in the K–12 environment, typically because they have something other than a learning disability); Section 504 plans sometimes offer different services and accommodations than are typically offered in an IEP.

Accommodation is the term for any adjustment that a college makes to its program that is designed to help students show what they know in spite of their disability (e.g., extended testing time); see Step 5.

An IEP is a formalized plan that IDEA requires K–12 schools to write for students with disabilities that outlines what services and accommodations the school will provide for them.

Disability Services (DS) Office is the office at college in charge of reviewing requests for accommodation and for coordinating those accommodations.

to identify students with disabilities, educate them in the most inclusive settings, or provide specialized instruction (McGuire, 2009). Instead, according to the law, colleges simply "must afford handicapped persons equal opportunity to obtain the same result, to gain the same benefit, or to reach the same level of achievement" (34 C.F.R. § 104.4[2]). Students who have been accustomed to significant modifications (e.g., a reduction in required page length for essays) may find these accommodations unavailable to them, as colleges might view such adaptations as going beyond simply providing access (Madaus, 2009). It makes sense that elementary and secondary school districts should provide more and different supports (e.g., providing specialized instruction); they have to take care of all students in the district, which involves serving a huge spectrum of needs. Colleges, on the other hand, only have to provide accommodations for students with disabilities who meet the entrance criteria and maintain the minimum GPA to stay enrolled (McGuire, 2009).

Providing Reasonable Accommodations

In the postsecondary environment, conversation about accommodations frequently centers on whether students' requested adjustments are "reasonable." Again, the emphasis of Section 504 and the ADA is on providing access to programs, not on making sure everyone who enrolls at the college can stay there, and these laws provide some guidance to help colleges determine what might not be reasonable adjustments. One of the stipulations the ADA specifically makes is that colleges do not have to make modifications that "would fundamentally alter the nature of the service, program, or activity" (28 C.F.R. §35.130[b][7]); this exception applies to tests, course requirements, requirements for majors, and graduation requirements. Certain accommodations may not be available to students, depending upon what skills are being measured by a test or class (Madaus, 2009). For instance, students taking a class where calculation is one of the skills being evaluated would probably not be allowed to use a calculator for exams. However, in a physics course, the use of a calculator

---

College Support Services at a Glance

Colleges do ...

- have to provide students with disabilities equal access to the curriculum ("level the playing field").
- have to provide "reasonable" accommodations to students with disabilities.

Colleges do not ...

- have to modify ("fundamentally alter") admission requirements, tests, course requirements, requirements for majors, or graduation requirements for students with disabilities.
- have to provide "personal services" to students with disabilities, such as specialized tutoring services.

might be considered reasonable—and this option actually might be available to every student in the class.

In a court case in the 1990s, Boston University asserted its right to require all students, regardless of whether or not they had a disability, to study a foreign language—and the district court agreed with the college (see box, "Rights in Motion at the College Level"). At the time, the court noted that refusal to make accommodations such as course waivers should occur only after a college goes through a deliberative process about the adjustment being requested and the school's essential requirements (Wolinsky & Whelan, 1999). But as long as a college has conducted such a review, it can elect to refuse certain kinds of accommodations.

Rights in Motion at the College Level: *Guckenberger v. Boston University* (1997)

Guckenberger is a landmark case in the field of disability law, and it is a great example of how the rights of students and colleges intersect at the college level. *Guckenberger* was a class action suit by students with learning disabilities (LD) and attention deficit disorders (ADD) against BU.

Although BU previously had approved substitutions for its foreign language graduation requirement, after a change in management at the DS office BU terminated all course substitutions. In addition, the university established a new rule requiring both incoming students and current students who had already been approved for support due to their learning disabilities to be retested if their documentation was more than 3 years old or was performed by professionals without the credentials specified by BU's DS office. The DS office grievance policy also was altered to prevent students from appealing to anyone but the provost (who had led the restaffing and set the tone for the DS office), and the office denied a variety of requests (Wolinsky & Whelan, 1999).

The court found that the school's requirements for approved LD evaluators were too inappropriately narrow and discriminatory. It criticized BU for its failure to notify students about its new documentation approval and grievance procedures, for the substance of its grievance procedures, for having unqualified staff make the accommodation decisions, and for taking too long to make them. BU's requirement that students be retested was found to be reasonable for students with ADD but not for students with LD. The court also found that BU could not unilaterally refuse all course substitution requests.

However, in a second opinion—after BU pulled together a faculty committee to discuss the school's foreign language policy—the court did support BU's right to refuse substitutions for foreign language. The university had shown that it had made this decision on the basis of discussions with relevant departments and administrators and had concluded that such a substitution would constitute a fundamental alteration to its programs. So, although course substitutions can be viewed as reasonable accommodations, in this case the substitution was deemed to represent a fundamental alteration to the university's program. In other words, the rights of colleges to keep their requirements intact essentially trumped the rights of students to a particular accommodation.

Section 504 and the ADA also say that schools do not have to grant accommodations that would create an "undue burden" for a school—financially or administratively (42 U.S.C. § 12112[b][5][A]). For instance, it would be considered unreasonable for a college to rearrange its entire class schedule in order to accommodate the needs of a student whose medication wears off by the afternoon; a more reasonable accommodation would be to allow the student to register earlier than most other students (i.e., *priority registration*) in order to allow him to schedule courses at the time of day when he's most effective. Colleges rarely claim undue financial burden, partially because other stipulations and exceptions in the law may resolve an issue. For example, colleges do have to provide sign language interpreting when appropriate for students with hearing impairments, even though this tends to be expensive. Colleges cannot claim that they can't afford to provide this accommodation because they must provide all students equal access to the school's curriculum and programs. However, colleges are not obligated to provide students with one-on-one tutoring—not because it's costly, but because it falls under the category of *personal services*, something the law says colleges don't have to provide (34 C.F.R. § 104.4[b][iii] and [iv]).

Federal law also says that colleges do not have to "permit an individual to participate in or benefit from the services, programs, or activities of that public entity when that individual poses a direct threat to the health or safety of others" (28 C.F.R. § 35.139). As they have to do when they consider whether an accommodation would represent a fundamental alteration, colleges have to make an individual decision about safety based on the particulars of a student's situation (e.g., current mental or physical state based on information provided by a professional who treats her, the requirements of the program or site placement) rather than on assumptions (e.g., all students with bipolar disorder would make bad psychologists). Colleges also have to consider whether some sort of reasonable accommodation might mitigate the threat (28 C.F.R. § 35.139). This exception is most likely to be raised in courses of study or field placements involving patient care; colleges and the professional organizations (e.g., hospitals) with which they work have to be careful that they do not place patients at risk for harm (see box, "Accommodations in Field Placements" on page 8). But it also may be raised when students who have made threats against others are expelled or put on a forced leave. Again, colleges cannot simply decide that every student diagnosed with antisocial personality disorder, for example, poses a direct threat to others. Instead, they must evaluate situations as they arise and look at the details of a particular student's condition and actions, rather than make decisions based on gross generalizations about the danger a student may pose.

The last stipulation is one that may affect more students. Federal law says that colleges don't have to "provide to individuals with disabilities personal devices, such as wheelchairs; individually prescribed devices, such as prescription eyeglasses or hearing aids; readers for personal use or study; or services of a personal nature including assistance in eating, toileting, or dressing" (28 C.F.R. § 35.135). Students who require personal assistance for needs other than learning (e.g., dressing themselves) will find that, although schools allow personal attendants to be present on campus, they are not required to provide or pay for such services.

Most students and parents understand this on a fundamental level; they would not expect a college to buy glasses for a student who needs them. However, they might be surprised at how this exception affects services to which students may be accustomed. For instance, although many colleges provide tutoring services (because college is a business, and schools want students' business), they are not required to provide specialized tutoring (e.g., compensatory techniques, reading comprehension instruction, multisensory instruction), tutoring in a one-on-one setting, or tutoring by a qualified professional. (At some schools, tutoring centers are staffed by undergraduate students.) Students who feel strongly that they need individualized supplemental instruction provided by experienced professionals must carefully research different colleges to make sure that the college they attend offers such a service (Banerjee & Brinckerhoff, 2009; McGuire, 2009; see Step 6 for more on researching college possibilities). Otherwise, students will have to pay for any tutoring they need.

Although colleges have to make certain accommodations available, how and when they make them available may also be an issue for college-bound students with disabilities. For instance, colleges are not required to provide round-the-clock access to specific kinds of **assistive technology** (see Step 5 for more on this). Most schools offer students access to equipment or software programs to help them with their reading or other academic tasks, such as speech-to-text software. But even if a school chooses to provide such technology, it does not have to provide students with the equipment and site licenses to use it in their dorm room. Schools typically have such software loaded on a few computers, perhaps in their DS office and in the library: Students may have to sign up for a session to use it, and it will not be available to them when the office or library is closed—and these locations are not required to extend their hours as an accommodation. Also, the college is within its rights to choose the brand of equipment or type of software program, as long as it is effective, so students cannot require that a college purchase the text-to-speech program that they got used to using in high school (Banerjee, 2009). Another example relates to sign language interpreting. Colleges have to provide this for any school-related occasion (such as

Accommodations in Field Placements

Martin Jakubowski, a medical resident with Asperger's syndrome, was removed from a family medicine residency program because his communication skills were so poor that nurses and others could not understand him (*Jakubowski v. Christ Hospital,* 2009). As an accommodation, he asked that those with whom he worked be made aware of his condition and its triggers. The hospital felt that this was an insufficient solution and that the only way to ensure patient safety would be to assign a doctor to oversee the resident's every move at the hospital, which the hospital viewed as an undue burden. The hospital terminated his family medicine residency and offered him a position in pathology, which Jakubowski refused. The court found in favor of the hospital, ruling that the resident was not otherwise qualified to complete the program in family medicine because the accommodations required to ensure patient safety were unreasonable.

a field trip or a performance offered on campus), but they do have to provide interpreters for students to chat with friends at the campus café.

Giving students and their families an understanding of the legal backdrop for college disability services provides a foundation for understanding how things work in that environment. In the best-case scenario, it will help to guide the IEP team in choosing adjustments that help to prepare a student for the college environment, where certain kinds of modifications may be unavailable. For students on 504 plans, it can help to educate them about how shifts within 504 apply to them in the transition to college.

Yet this information may also cause some families to become concerned about how the limitations of certain kinds of accommodation might affect students. And, despite the information supplied by such an overview of the law, some families might still have misconceptions about how supportive the college support services will be. This is why students and their families also need to become familiar with what the research says about students' experiences at college. Some might be surprised by what it says about what makes students successful.

The Research on Students With Disabilities in the College Setting

Most of the research conducted regarding college students is qualitative; the truth is that the field does not provide much in the way of data. Colleges are, for the most part, independent entities and they have limited responsibilities with regard to tracking their students with disabilities, as federal law does not require of them the same kind of extensive recordkeeping that it does schools in the K-to-12 system. Although the decentralized nature of the postsecondary world makes it difficult to collect data, in 2008 roughly 11% of students enrolled at college claimed to have a disability (U.S. Government Accountability Office, 2009).

Skinner & Lindstrom (2003) identified characteristics of students with disabilities who were successful at college. These characteristics are the same as those identified by professionals from various sectors of the education field (e.g. college disability services [DS], school counseling) as qualities successful students possess (Banerjee & Brinckerhoff, 2009; Martin, Portley, & Graham, 2009; Milsom & Dietz, 2009; Skinner & Lindstrom, 2003; Smitley, 2000):

- Knowledge of their disabilities and of appropriate compensation strategies.

- Self-advocacy skills.

Definition

Assistive technology refers to various assistive, adaptive, and rehabilitative devices, generally electronic or computerized.

- The ability to organize their time, materials, and assignments.

- Coping skills to handle academic responsibilities and other aspects of their lives.

- The will to set goals and the skills to make a plan to meet them (*self-determination*).

- Motivation.

- Confidence.

- Persistence/perseverance.

- Resilience.

- Self-discipline.

- Support networks.

- Use of learning strategies.

- Use of accommodations.

Some of these qualities are internal and are part and parcel of students' personalities. Others are skills that can be taught or are characteristics that might be developed through such techniques as reward systems and consistent external feedback.

Unfortunately, studies show that many students with disabilities at college are not prepared for the responsibility of managing their academic work and their lives (Sitlington, 2003; Smith, English, & Vasek, 2002). They do not know how to make good use of their time and are overwhelmed by the workload (Sitlington, 2003; Smith et al., 2002). Many lack independence, and they miss the academic support that they received from their parents throughout their lives (Janiga & Costenbader, 2002; Smith et al., 2002). They also

- struggle with distractions (Smith et al., 2002);

- lack self-advocacy skills (Janiga & Costenbader, 2002; Smith et al., 2002);

- do not have strategies for learning and independent study skills (Brinckerhoff, 1996; Lock & Layton, 2001; Sitlington, 2003);

- do not understand their own profile of learning strengths and weaknesses (Brinckerhoff, 1996; Janiga & Costenbader, 2002; Lock & Layton, 2001; Skinner, 2004);

- cannot explain their disability, and do not know what accommodations would be appropriate for their learning issues (Janiga & Costenbader, 2002); and

- lack the skills to recognize when they need help and how to seek it when they do (Brinckerhoff, 1996; Lock & Layton, 2001).

Some students with disabilities can be passive learners who do not see a connection between ordinary academic tasks such as keeping up with reading and taking notes and academic success (Lock & Layton, 2001). Their writing and reading skills may lack the sophistication to meet the expectations of the college environment (Brinckerhoff, 1996; Janiga & Costenbader, 2002). The concerns are numerous and wide-ranging, covering students' academic preparation as well as their general self-sufficiency.

This list of worries about students' preparedness can seem overwhelming. But these concerns coalesce into several overarching themes. The most commonly repeated suggestions for success (Brinckerhoff, 1996; Janiga & Costenbader, 2002; McGuire, 2009; Milsom & Dietz, 2009; Sitlington, 2003; Skinner, 2004; Skinner & Lindstrom, 2003; Smith et al., 2002; Webb, Patterson, Syverud, & Seabrooks-Blackmore, 2008; Wilson, Hoffman, & McLaughlin, 2009) are that students with disabilities should:

1. Know about disability protection laws in effect for students at the college level and how these affect their rights.

2. Know about disability services and how to access them.

3. Know about the differences between the high school and college settings.

4. Have the proper academic preparation.

5. Be ready to self-advocate.

Development of these skills must begin early in high school so that students are fully prepared for success at college (Faggella-Luby, Flannery, & Simonsen, 2009).

The Research on Accommodations

Prevatt, Johnson, Allison, and Proctor (2005) surveyed students who were identified with learning disabilities after they had enrolled at college. The accommodations that were used by at least 50% of the students and received the highest ratings of usefulness from the students were:

1. Registering with the university DS office or center (a necessity in order to receive accommodations).

2. Course waiver or course substitution.

3. Study aids.

4. Increased time spent studying or preparing for class.

5. Creating examples of the applicable material for study purposes.

6. Sitting in the front of the class.

7. Informing the professor about the disability.

8. Learning how to reason through an answer.

9. Using all auditory, visual, and kinesthetic modalities.

10. Keeping a planner.

What is interesting about this list of items—referred to in the study (Prevatt et al., 2005) as *accommodations*—is that most of these are strategies that students utilize on their own, rather than adjustments colleges make to their tests or requirements. This point should be noted by all members of IEP teams—professionals, parents, and students—so that they place as much emphasis on strategies and skills that students can use on their own as they do on classroom-based accommodations. The least frequently used accommodations were:

1. Taking a study-skills class.

2. Getting training in relaxation techniques.

3. Getting a tutor.

4. Getting counseling for emotional issues.

Although the study's structure did not allow for responses on each of these items individually, students said that they did not use certain accommodations because they were not interested, thought that they were a waste of time, had tried them before and found them ineffective, or were overwhelmed by the number of recommendations that evaluating professionals had made for them (Prevatt et al., 2005).

Hadley (2006) suggested that students do not use certain accommodations because of the time—and, in some cases, the monetary—investment. While they are still in high school, students need to learn how to undertake some of these activities that take time to learn so that they will have the skills in place before they get to college. Students new to college and feeling overwhelmed by the amount of work they have to do will be less likely to invest time in learning strategies while they are struggling to keep up with their class content (see box, "The Professional Connection").

It should be noted as well that students who use more accommodations than others are not necessarily at an advantage. Trammell (2003) wondered whether a link could be drawn between accommodation use and improved grades, and found that students who had both learning disabilities and attention deficit disorder (ADD) showed significant grade improvements associated with their accommodation use, whereas students with learning disabilities only did worse as their number of accommodations increased. Trammell noted that the mean grades of students with lower verbal SAT scores (an indicator, perhaps, of more severe learning disabilities) fell with each additional accommodation they used. He theorized that much of this discrepancy between their grades and those of the students with ADD was due to the appropriateness (or lack of appropriateness) of the accommodations that students chose for themselves, and that the processing abilities of the students with learning disabilities may have made it more difficult for them to choose effective accommodations for themselves.

The Research on College Preparedness

One of the themes that emerge from the research on students with disabilities attending college is that they need to know what to expect once they get there. All freshmen find themselves in a new world when they arrive at college, but for students with disabilities the stress of the environment can be more challenging. All college-bound students benefit from knowing what to expect, of course, but it is especially important that students with disabilities—whose areas of weakness may be specifically challenged by the changes—understand the college environment long before they arrive there (see Step 2 for more on this).

The Professional Connection

Students—with and without disabilities—are frequently overwhelmed by the adjustments they have to make to their study and reading habits when they get to college. Students with disabilities that affect their learning will be even more affected by both the environment and the demands. The research shows that students at college don't want to spend time learning how to use technology or study techniques—yet the research also says that these things can be of great help. This is why training in the use of relevant technologies and direct instruction in learning and study strategies and strategies that bypass students' disabilities should be a major part of students' programming in high school. This way, they will not have to spend precious study time simply learning how to use the techniques and technology that will make studying easier.

Hadley (2006) held focus groups and conducted interviews to get students' perspectives on their readiness and development as college students. The experiences of students with learning disabilities echoed the findings of other studies. Not surprisingly, many described their academic struggles. Some noted problems keeping up with their reading assignments, others with managing their assignments (i.e., prioritizing and knowing how to start). Students expressed surprise at the extent of the writing demands (with regard to the number of assignments and the rigorous expectations for them) and, at the same time, how few assignments there were overall (a disadvantage for those who were poor test takers and those who relied on teacher comments as a gauge of whether or not they were mastering the material).

Students in Hadley's study (2006) reported meeting with professors as a way of finding a starting point for assignments. They also often needed to ask professors for help even after visiting tutoring centers, having found the tutors to be of limited assistance. In addition, some students were not happy with their accommodations: They had had difficulty knowing where they were to take their accommodated exams, and those who took them outside of the class regretted their lack of access to professors.

The students in Skinner's study (2004) stressed the importance of understanding their learning disabilities and having strategies to circumvent them—something all of the students reported doing. Most had vague memories of someone explaining their psychoeducational evaluation to them, but they did not appear to have gained or retained much from these conversations. All of the students found value in the accommodations they received for their learning disabilities, and yet not one of them demonstrated specific knowledge about their legal rights or responsibilities. The graduates felt that their support systems (i.e., family, friends, and help sources on campus) were vital in helping them succeed. And they also endorsed the necessity of goal setting and perseverance.

Summary

Although all students headed to college should have an understanding of the environment they are entering and the changes it entails, such preparation is even more critical for students with disabilities. The discussion about the differences in the college environment needs to begin early in high school, so that students can make an educated decision about whether or not college is the postsecondary goal for which they really want to prepare. Most high school students with disabilities (and their classmates without disabilities, too) are not ready to make big, life-directing decisions. Many will simply follow the typical path to college, because they want to, or because they think it's what they're supposed to do (or both). For these students, preparation should begin in freshman year or beforehand to make sure that they are ready for the environment. The steps that follow this one will help to guide the development of the skills students need to be successful at college.

Step 2

Know Student Rights and Responsibilities

Probably the biggest change that all students experience when they transition to college is the amount of responsibility and independence that they have. They find themselves in charge of everything: completing paperwork, registering for classes, doing laundry, and so forth. This is because students at college, even those who are not yet 18, are considered adults. As adults, they also enjoy an amount of freedom (e.g., to stay up as late as they want, to eat when they choose, etc.). In addition, the Family Educational Rights and Privacy Act of 1974 (FERPA) offers college students adult-level privacy: While they are in college, their grades and any records relating to academics and behavior cannot (with a few exceptions) be shared without the student's permission (e.g., grades don't get sent to the parents, even if they are paying the bill). Students need to be prepared for the obligations and freedoms they will find at college, and to be aware of their rights in the college environment.

Step 2

Know Student Rights and Responsibilities

Students with disabilities at college are treated the same way as their peers with regard to the expectation that they will be responsible for themselves—and they, too, are entitled to the same freedoms and privacy as their peers without disabilities. However, unlike their classmates who don't have disabilities, students who want accommodations must assume additional responsibilities in order to receive accommodations. This is because the law doesn't require colleges to identify students with learning disabilities and offer them services (McGuire, 2009). Also, because colleges cannot require students to disclose their disability in the admission process (34 C.F.R. § 104.42[c]), they don't know which of their students has a disability. As with other typical elements of college life, the disability services (DS) system is one that mixes students' rights with their responsibilities (see box, "Student Rights and Responsibilities at a Glance").

Student Rights and Responsibilities at a Glance

- The decision to apply for accommodations and services belongs to students; colleges cannot make them self-identify and will not offer services to students who do not self-identify.

- The application of FERPA at the college level means that information about students' actual diagnosis will generally be kept private by college staff unless the student asks for the information to be disclosed or there is a safety concern.

- Students can file a grievance for a variety of issues related to their treatment as individuals with disabilities (or if they are found ineligible for such a designation).

- Because students with disabilities must be treated in the same way as their peers, they are subject to the same disciplinary and honor code rules and subject to the same punishment if they commit an infraction.

Rights

Right to Privacy

Colleges are subject to the Federal Educational Rights and Privacy Act (FERPA), which is designed to protect students' educational records from being disclosed inappropriately. However, even though students' documentation is often filed in the Disability Services office (rather than in the dean's or registrar's office), it is legally considered part of the student's educational record (which includes transcripts and other information relevant to students' enrollment at the college). Even so, colleges neither casually pass these records around to professors nor typically grant just any professor or other college personnel who asks for it permission to see the records without student approval. Notification about students' approved accommodations is provided through the Letter of Accommodation (LOA), which does not typically reveal anything about students' disability.

Faculty or staff members who, for whatever reason, want to see a student's disability documentation must demonstrate a "legitimate educational interest" (34 CFR § 99.31), and some colleges contend that professors generally meet this requirement (Legal Roundup, 2008c). A recent policy guidance statement from the U.S. Department of Education (2004) noted that documentation of disability on file at a college could be disclosed to faculty without students' permission, but it left the door open for colleges to establish policies that are more stringent. Read the government's guidance at:

www.ed.gov/policy/gen/guid/fpco/ferpa/library/copeuna.html

> *Note: Colleges really do not place a big burden on students when it comes to the accommodation request process and any processes related to receiving their accommodations. Most students will be able to handle these few additional responsibilities. Those who cannot deal with these procedures will likely find themselves doing without their accommodations, as the law holds them responsible for initiating the accommodation process and for following through with any parts of the process assigned to them.*
>
> *Federal law expects students with disabilities to take responsibility for themselves at college, as they are considered adults. But this does not mean that they are without protection. The ADA and Section 504 were written to make sure that students with disabilities would receive the same access to college programs that their classmates without disabilities do. Students need to know what these rights are so that, if necessary, they can assert them with the confidence that they know how the law protects them.*

DS providers do respect students' privacy, and they do their part to protect it. Although there is no guarantee that colleges will enact a restrictive policy when it comes to disclosure, many schools will not open students' DS files without their permission for just anyone on the faculty without serious consideration of that person's "legitimate educational interest" or the seriousness of the situation (i.e., an emergency situation). However, each school has its own disclosure rules, so students who are concerned about who will have access to their records should ask about this during their college search.

Professors, too, are expected to respect students' privacy. They should not single students out in front of their classmates or comment on their need for accommodation. At some schools, the opportunity to volunteer as a notetaker is announced by professors, who might read a short statement at the beginning of class saying something like, "Anyone who would like to volunteer as a notetaker for a student with special needs in this class should contact DS." The professor should not name the student who needs the notetaker or in any way reveal the identity of the student. Students who feel that their professors have violated their privacy rights should discuss the violation with DS; this is a situation where it would be appropriate for DS to intervene.

Students' privacy rights extend to their transcripts, which will not carry any notation or indication that students have utilized services as federal law forbids it (Legal Roundup, 2009c). Some students worry that the records they request to have sent to graduate schools to which they are applying might include information about their accommodations. This information, which is part of students' record while they are at college, will not be sent to another school or employer by their college unless they specifically request this. If students take remedial courses (which many students without disabilities also have to take), these will be listed on their transcripts. But their transcript will neither have a designation to show that they received accommodations nor list what the accommodations were. The U.S. Department of Education produced a pamphlet to educate students with disabilities about their rights and responsibilities at college. It can be read and/or downloaded at:

    www2.ed.gov/about/offices/list/ocr/transition.html

Right to Receive Accommodations in a Reasonable Amount of Time

Once students are approved for accommodations (and, as previously noted, have met their obligations to procedures and timelines), the accommodations must be delivered in a timely manner. Although it is "reasonable" for it to take a few days to get notetakers assigned or get copies of text in an alternative format, the delay in making arrangements can't be too long, or schools will be in danger of denying students their access to college classes (Legal Roundup, 2010b).

Right to Individual Review of Requests

As Step 1 discussed, requests for accommodation must be reviewed based on individual circumstances—the student's disabling condition, its severity, and the course in which it is being requested. This means, for example, that colleges should not have a standard list of accommodations that they grant to students with attention deficit disorders (ADD), as all students with ADD do not experience the same symptoms. Likewise, requests for certain significant accommodations (e.g., waiver of the foreign language requirement) should not be rejected outright unless the college has undergone a deliberative process and determined them to be fundamental alterations. In addition, professors should not refuse to allow an accommodation without going through the process to establish that it would represent a fundamental alteration (such a review may involve their department head, DS, and other officers of the college). But until such a determination has been reached, professors cannot deny students accommodations approved by the DS office.

Right to Register a Grievance

When students have difficulty relating to accommodations, it is usually better to try to work things out with professors or other college staff members by themselves, and to call on DS staff only if this does not work (see box, "Reasons to Grieve"). All students—with and without disabilities—need to learn how to work out conflicts in a mature and effective manner. However, if they can't make progress with

Reasons to Grieve

There are several reasons why a student might wish to file a grievance:

- When the college decides a student is not eligible for services, despite a longstanding diagnosis and accommodation (see more on this in Step 5).

- When a student who is eligible for services does not receive all of the requested accommodations, or the college substitutes what it considers to be more reasonable accommodations for those that were initially requested (see more on this in Step 5).

- When something outside the student's control interferes with the proper delivery of an accommodation.

- When students feel that they have been a victim of discrimination on the basis of their disability.

Most students will never have any cause to file a grievance. For those who think that they do, information about the college's procedures for this should be easily found on its web site, often as a link from the DS homepage. Before they leave for college, students should be aware that such a process exists, so that they feel secure about the protection of their rights.

their professors or feel that professors are too hostile, they should seek help from DS, which may be able to apply an appropriate amount of pressure to resolve the problem. If the DS staff has been unable to help—or when the problem concerns a member of DS staff—students need to know that they can pursue a complaint in a more formal way. There are three potential routes for this. Students can

- Go through the college's grievance procedure,

- Complain to the U.S. Department of Education's Office for Civil Rights (OCR), which oversees issues regarding disability and discrimination), or

- File a lawsuit.

Going through the college's grievance process is usually the fastest route to a resolution. It will involve fewer people and, in most cases, there will not be a backlog of other complaints that have to be resolved first. Students may have to complete a form, make an appointment, or send an e-mail to initiate the grievance process, and a member of the college staff will follow up. Students who want to go through OCR will have to follow similar procedures. Find your local OCR enforcement office at:

 http://wdcrobcolp01.ed.gov/CFAPPS/OCR/contactus.cfm

No matter which of these routes they choose (and they do not have to go through the college's process before going to OCR), students should know that certain things can bring an investigation to a halt. The first one is the statute of limitations. Every college and OCR office will have a set number of days during which students can file a complaint, and grievances filed after the statute of limitations will likely not be pursued. Another reason investigations sometimes end quickly is because students have failed to follow the proper procedures. For instance, if a college requires students to give 5 days' notice of a need for exam accommodations, and the appointed college official or OCR discovers that a student did not request an accommodation until the day of the exam, it is likely that the complaint will simply be closed at that point. Even when they meet all of the technical requirements for filing a grievance, students should know that, when it comes to arguments about accommodations versus essential elements of classes or programs, courts tend to side with colleges (McGuire, 2009).

As far as a lawsuit goes, there is an obvious expense involved, and the timeline is probably the longest of the three options. A recent complaint against Princeton University by a freshman with learning disabilities (*Metcalf-Leggette v. Princeton*, 2009) makes this clear. Even though the student initiated legal proceedings early in the semester, she had to take her first semester midterms and finals without the extended time that she had requested, because of the length of the process. Either of the other two routes described will be much more expedient than going to court.

Responsibilities

Responsibility: Accessing Services and Accommodations

Students with disabilities who want to receive services and accommodations have to take responsibility for registering with the DS office and for completing some minor tasks once they do so. The process for requesting accommodations at college is not onerous, but students are solely responsible for initiating the process. This is an example of the mixing of rights and responsibilities: Students have the freedom to keep the disability from becoming part of their identity at college (see box, "Deciding to Self-Identify"; also see Step 5 for more on this), but if they want accommodations, they must be responsible for completing the process of applying for them.

Deciding to Self-Identify

One freedom that students with disabilities at college can exercise is their right not to be officially identified as having a disability. Despite what may be a long history of receiving services throughout their education, students can come to college and never officially let anyone know that they have a disability. Obviously, the apparent presence of a disability makes this more challenging for those with physical manifestations than for those with "hidden" disabilities like attention deficit disorders, autism spectrum disorder, or psychological disabilities. But even students with the most severe disabilities can opt not to register for services.

Students should understand that, although the decision to self-identify is their choice, they have to be prepared to live with the consequences of such a choice. This means that they have to live with any bad grades they earn without their accommodations (McGuire, 2009). Even if they apply for accommodations right after their first exams and are quickly approved, they will not be allowed to retake those exams, and their grades will not be expunged (McGuire, 2009). Some students with disabilities are not good at predicting the outcome of their actions, and some may not have a realistic perception of how much they are helped by their accommodations. As Step 3 will discuss, preparing for the transition to college must include activities to enhance self-knowledge and awareness of the status of students' disability, in order to make the most appropriate decision regarding requesting accommodations.

There are real-life implications of making such decisions. Abandoning all educational supports might result in a disastrous academic performance. College accommodations for students with disabilities is another example of how freedom and responsibility intertwine at college, as students bear the full responsibility for what happens if they choose not to request accommodations.

Most colleges inform incoming freshmen and transfer students of the existence of a DS office or staff person and include information about DS in student handbooks; some send letters describing services with the acceptance letter, and others even hold information sessions during freshman orientation. However, the law does not require colleges to reach out to students with disabilities beyond such notifications, nor does it require them to figure out who on their campus has a disability and offer them services. Even if students disclose their disability during the admissions process, either by writing their essay about it or by including their disability documentation with their application, most colleges will not consider this to be sufficient notification (Madaus, 2009). The admissions office is unlikely to forward any information it receives during the application process to DS (except at schools where students are simultaneously applying for a special program for students with disabilities). And even if Admissions does forward the information, the DS office is unlikely to act on it, because it is the student's responsibility to initiate the accommodation process.

Learn About the Process

Every college has its own procedures for requesting accommodations. The first step should be accessing the DS office's page of the college web site, which may outline the process or at the very least will have contact information (see Step 6). The process might begin by calling to set up an appointment, or by sending an e-mail providing general information. Some DS offices want students to present their documentation in person, whereas others prefer it be mailed or dropped off at the DS office; students may also have to complete a form that asks them questions about their diagnosis, how it affects their functioning, and what accommodations they wish to request.

Students must complete all of the steps of the accommodation request process in order to receive services (Step 5 talks about the process more fully, and Step 7 discusses paperwork in more detail), and DS offices are not responsible for following up with them if they only complete some of the steps. For instance, if a school's process requires that students submit their documentation and meet with a coordinator, and a student only submits her paperwork and requests and doesn't make an appointment, then DS will likely place her documentation in a file but they will not call her to ask her to finish the process, and they will not grant her accommodations until she does what she is supposed to do. Similarly, if she submits her documentation but does not request accommodations, DS might follow up with her to ask what she wants, but they do not have to do so. Again, they will likely place her information in a file and wait for her to return with her requests (see box, "DS and the Parent Connection" on page 23).

The process for requesting accommodations at college is not difficult; it is simply another procedure students have to follow like so many others at school, such as registration for classes. Because students at college maintain certain rights and freedoms, they can even choose not to engage in this process, as long as they are ready to take responsibility for their actions (see Step 5).

Communicate With Professors

At many colleges, students are responsible for at least part, if not all, of the process for notifying professors of their approval for accommodations, but these procedures are not that difficult or time-consuming (Madaus, 2009). Most college DS offices generate a LOA that students use to inform professors what accommodations have been approved for them (see Figure 2-1 on page 24). Typically, students are responsible for retrieving these letters from the DS office and delivering them to their professors (Madaus, 2009). Some schools require students to have the professors sign the letters (as proof that they have seen them) and return them to DS. Note that the LOA usually does not provide details about the student's disability. Of course, if students wish to disclose their diagnosis to a professor, there is nothing to stop them from doing this, and some DS offices encourage such disclosures when students are comfortable making them (see Step 4).

Even in the age of technology, many colleges are sticking to hard copies of letters rather than e-mailing notifications to professors, due to concerns about privacy, a desire to give students the freedom to decide whom they want notified, and to ensure that students assume responsibility for this process. Many DS offices consider themselves a backup for this communication rather than the vehicle for it.

DS and the Parent Connection

"Hello. This is Elizabeth Hamblet's mother. I'd like to know whether she came to your office to get her accommodations. If she didn't, I'd like to send you her paperwork and put in her requests."

DS offices at colleges all across the country receive calls like this. The answer parents receive will depend up on the philosophy of the college's DS office. Some offices will refuse to speak to parents at all without students' permission, so it may be a very short conversation. Others might not give out any information about the particular student, but will instead share with parents the process that students have to follow to get accommodations and ask parents to contact their student with the information. Some might even offer to contact students and let them know that their parents were asking about them coming in for services. But parents should know that colleges are not obligated to do any of these things, and only in a very specific circumstance where parents have guardianship can they make the accommodation requests. Parents should remember that DS offices are charged with protecting—for better or for worse—students' privacy, and they don't refuse to allow parent requests or give out information because they are mean or don't like parents.
Parents' best bet is to work with their student and the high school to make sure that their student leaves for college ready to ask for accommodations and prepared for whatever the procedures require.

Figure 2-1. Letter of Accommodation

Disability Services Office
123 Administration Building, Anycollege, USA
T (999) 555-0000 F (999) 555-1111

**Hamblet
University**

Letter of Accommodation

Student Name:_____Semester: _____

Today's date: _____Valid from: _____ through:_____

Federal legislation including the Americans with Disabilities Act and Section 504 of the Rehabilitation Act states that academically qualified students with disabilities must be reasonably accommodated in instruction and academic assessment. A *disability* is legally defined as a physical or mental impairment substantially limiting one or more major life activities.

This letter verifies that the above-named student has undergone a needs assessment with Disabilities Services and it was determined that he/she has a disability requiring the academic accommodations or services listed below.

The accommodations checked below are those to which this student is entitled:

❑   Extended testing time

❑   Reduced-noise testing environment

❑   Word processing for essay tests

❑   Notetaker

❑   Use of device for recording lectures

❑   Interpreter, ASL, for lectures and oral exams

❑   Electronic books or books on tape

DS accommodations are intended to provide equal access as required by law. Revisions to accommodations may occur pending additional information, changes in disability status, or by periodic review. Faculty is encouraged to work collaboratively with the student and to seek support from DS as needed. Please contact DS with questions or concerns regarding the provision of accommodations and services.

Responsibility: Managing Accommodations

Students usually need to provide the DS office with a list of their classes and professors *each semester*. DS offices are not responsible for contacting students every semester to find out whether or not they want their accommodations; the responsibility for making the request lies with the student (Legal Roundup, 2008b). Some offices will follow up when students do not ask for their accommodation letters at the beginning of the semester, but others will not, and there is no legal obligation for them to do so. When students who did not ask for accommodations in a particular semester later complain that they were denied their rights, the complaint investigations generally find in favor of colleges.

Students may have some responsibilities beyond delivering their LOAs. For instance, they may have to sign a form and turn it in a few days before they need accommodations on an exam. They may have to research the requirements for a field placement so that DS can help to arrange any accommodations they may need. Because students are responsible for themselves, their failure to complete procedures can result in their not receiving accommodations (Legal Roundup, 2009b). Not only do students have to complete procedures for accommodation, but they also must do so in their university's established timeline. This makes sense, as it can take a while to make different kinds of arrangements (e.g., hiring a sign language interpreter for a field trip).

In addition to requesting their LOA each semester, students are also responsible for *requesting more or different accommodations* if they find that the ones they are receiving are not helpful (Madaus, 2009). This is not to say that accommodations for which they were first denied will automatically be granted if they feel their current accommodations are not working. Rather, this means that it is the student's responsibility to alert DS if the approved accommodations are not sufficient (Madaus, 2009). Every year, students file grievances against DS offices claiming that they were denied their rights because they did not receive particular accommodations or because the ones they did receive were not helpful. In some of these cases, investigators discover that students did not actually request the accommodations in question or that they failed to inform DS that the ones they had were not helpful—and then they typically either dismiss the complaints or find in favor of the universities (Legal Roundup, 2009a).

DS procedures also require students to notify DS of their need for accommodations for each occasion that arises during the semester, and to do this within a designated time frame. For instance, students who need extended time for their exams may be required to send an e-mail or turn in a form signed by professors to DS 2 weeks in advance of exam dates so that DS can find proctors, locate rooms, and arrange to get the exams from professors in a secure manner (see box, "A Word About Exam Accommodations" on page 26). Students who fail to notify DS within this time frame or who do not do this at all might not receive their accommodations for those exams, as DS may legitimately not have enough time to arrange them (Legal Roundup, 2009a). When students who have "dropped the ball" file a grievance, the case will likely be dismissed or decided in favor of the college once it is discovered that students failed to meet the deadline established by DS procedures, unless there is an extenuating circumstance (e.g., student is hit by a car).

It's also students' responsibility to *notify DS of problems accessing accommodations. Sometimes*

- A professor gives a pop quiz, and he tells students that they do not need extra time for such a quick assessment.

- Students who have been approved for testing in a reduced-distractions location find that the room in which they are being tested has unreasonable noise or distractions.

- Students for whom a special lab table has been purchased find that it has been removed from the lab.

All of these situations warrant a resolution, but students have to inform DS of the problems, and they have to do so in a certain amount of time (the college's grievance procedures outline the statute of limitations; Legal Roundup, 2007). Students are responsible for letting DS know of any interference with their accommodations, regardless of whether the interference is intentional or accidental; it is not professors' responsibility, and DS will not contact students after every exam to see how things went. Once students report a problem, they may have to provide more information, but it will be DS's job to follow up with professors or building maintenance staff.

Responsibility: Purchasing Materials

All students are responsible for purchasing their textbooks, even if these are in alternative formats. DS will convert texts to the approved alternative format free of charge if they are not available directly from the publisher in an accessible format (Legal Roundup, 2010a), but—just like their peers without disabilities—students with disabilities must purchase the books in order to have them converted. Unfortunately, this means that students who have their books converted will lose the ability to resell them in a subsequent semester, as the conversion process usually involves removing

A Word About Exam Accommodations

At some colleges, DS may be not even be involved in exam accommodation arrangements, leaving it up to students and professors to work out details such as exam location and timing (Madaus, 2009). If this is their college's procedure, students can usually ask for some assistance from DS, especially in their first semester, but DS will not generally take over the process for students. It is considered reasonable for college students to have a hand in arranging their own accommodations.

books' bindings; this is one of many reasons for the movement to make textbooks more widely available in alternative formats. The point is that all students, regardless of whether or not they have disabilities, have to purchase some form of the texts. Students whose texts require conversion will have to get the books to DS in accordance with DS timelines so the converted texts are ready when they need them. Students cannot wait a month into the semester to get their books to DS and then complain that they did not receive their converted texts in time for the first few weeks of classes.

The same holds true for equipment. For instance, if students in a medical-related program are responsible for buying their own stethoscopes, students with hearing disabilities who need amplified stethoscopes are responsible for purchasing these. DS can help them locate distributors who sell such devices, but students have to buy their required materials, just as their classmates without disabilities do.

Responsibility: Following the Rules

Students with disabilities are expected to handle all of the responsibilities required of all students at college, including timely registration for classes (see box, "A Word About Deadlines"), completing forms related to enrollment, attending classes, and so on. Accommodations may be made for students with certain kinds of functional limitations (e.g., students with cerebral palsy will have assistance in completing certain forms that they are physically incapable of completing themselves) and students who suffer acute episodes related to their disability may be allowed some flexibility in class attendance (as is sometimes the case for students with psychological or medical problems). But generally, students who cannot fulfill the everyday responsibilities for typical college students at their institution may be considered not qualified to attend that college.

Like their peers without disabilities, students with disabilities are expected to adhere to their college's honor code and avoid committing behavioral and/or legal infractions. In the case of an infraction, the college might consider whether students' disability contributed to the violation, and it might seek advice from DS, but it will likely handle these students in the same way it would students without a disability. This treatment

A Word About Deadlines

Students should know, before they leave for college, what an add/drop deadline is and why they need to pay attention to it. This cut-off sets a final date for when students can either add a class to their schedule after the semester has begun or drop a class without the class and its accompanying grade appearing on their transcript. Because students with disabilities are rarely "allowed" to fail courses in high school, they may not recognize the need to drop a class before a very low grade compromises their GPA. They should know that the deadline for add/drop is the same for all students, regardless of disability, and put it on their calendar.

may be different from what students have experienced in high school. Although high schools have to follow special rules pertaining to disciplinary actions against students with disabilities and have to find appropriate placements for students who cannot learn in their typical environments, colleges are not bound by any such rules. They must treat students with disabilities the same way they treat all other students, in all positive and negative respects. If students do not meet their college's requirements for academics, behavior, and honor, they can be dismissed. So, although in general students' right to nondiscriminatory treatment is positive, they should know that this also means that they will be held just as accountable for their actions as any other student on campus.

Summary

Students enrolled at college are legally treated like adults. As such, the law requires them to take on certain responsibilities for completing procedures in order to get the accommodations they need. And the law also affords them certain protections. Students must come to college aware of both their obligations (so that they are prepared for what they will have to do) and their rights (so that no one can violate them).

Step 3

Develop Essential Personal Skills

Once the lessons of the research have been reviewed and understood and students understand how they will have to function in the college environment, the next step to college success is for them to acquire the skills needed to handle their responsibilities and assert their rights in an appropriate, effective way. As demonstrated by personal experience (see Epilogue) and research, students who are successful at college share certain characteristics directly related to personal skills (i.e., self-determination and self-advocacy). It is essential for college-bound high school students to develop self-management and these skill areas in order to be successful.

Step 3

Develop Essential Personal Skills

All college freshmen have to make adjustments when they leave home for college, and many students—with and without disabilities—find it difficult to adapt to being self-sufficient. Yet the college environment requires them to be totally independent in their functioning, completing big assignments without anyone checking on their progress, meeting paperwork deadlines for a variety of important events (such as registering for classes), choosing a schedule of courses that meet graduation requirements (with little assistance), and managing the nonacademic portions of their life (such as completing forms for the housing lottery).

Colleges hold the same expectations for students with and without disabilities, so although disability services (DS) offices help students with accommodations, they are not responsible for assisting them with their other college responsibilities, such as choosing an appropriate major or selecting classes to help them graduate with the required coursework. Students must know what kinds of questions to ask and how to request the help they may need to make the educated decisions they will have to make at college. This why it is important for students with disabilities to participate in their educational decision-making and support-provision processes during high school, and to develop the skills they will need to navigate the world beyond (Banerjee & Brinckerhoff, 2009; Kochhar-Bryant, Basset, & Webb, 2009; Madaus, 2009; Shaw, 2009; Wehmeyer & Schalock, 2001).

Students at college have to do many things independently, and there may be little or no specialized advising available to help them make very important decisions (e.g., choice of major, career field). At most schools, academic advisors do not have background knowledge about disabilities. Although DS staff may be willing to offer advice based on what they know about students' functioning, it is still up to students to choose a major whose requirements they can complete with "reasonable" accommodations (Madaus, 2009).

It is crucial for students to know themselves well and understand how to establish appropriate goals and work toward achieving them. In the research on success at college, students with disabilities have reported that **self-determination** skills have been instrumental to their success (Getzel & Thoma, 2008; Morningstar et al., 2010).

What Is Self-Determination?

Wehmeyer and Schalock (2001) defined *self-determination* as comprising certain skills and characteristics, including:

- decision making;

- problem solving;

- goal setting and attainment;

- self-observation, evaluation, and reinforcement;

- internal locus of control;

- positive attributions of efficacy and outcome expectancy;

- self-awareness; and

- self-knowledge.

These are skills that all adults, regardless of whether or not they have a disability, need in order to be successful. Throughout our life span we will make plans—we will set goals, figure out what skills or materials we need to accomplish them (and what support or help we might need), monitor our progress, handle some conflicts along the way, and, at the end of the line, evaluate any failures or shortcomings—and give ourselves credit for the things we have done correctly. Students need to develop and practice these skills while they are in high school so that they are ready to put them to use in the college environment.

Assessing Self-Determination Skills

Some schools assess students' self-determination skills through portfolio assessment (Field & Hoffman, 2007); this enables them to track students' progress through various projects. It can be helpful, though—and even more appropriate—for students to take the lead in self-assessment, using a self-determination scale such as the AIR Self-Determination Scale on page 43 (Wolman, Campeau, DuBois, Mithaug, & Stolarski, 1994; see pp. 54–61). Additional self-determination assessment tools are available at:

http://www.ou.edu/content/education/centers-and-partnerships/zarrow/self-determination-assessment-tools.html

---

Definition

Self-determination comprises the ability to set goals and the skills to make a plan to meet them, execute the plan, and reflect on plan's outcome.

How Can Students Develop Self-Determination?

Practice. There is a variety of self-determination curricula that can be part of a student's education plan, but students also need natural, real-life opportunities to practice these skills. At home, high school students can start by assuming responsibility for making and following a plan to purchase something they want, helping to develop shopping lists and buying groceries for the family, and participating in plans for family trips or activities, using a budget determined by their parents. Although these examples may seem unrelated to self-determination in college, these activities incorporate all of the relevant skills (and they have the benefit of having future usefulness in students' life). Visit:

www.sdsp.uncc.edu/pdf/curriculum_components.pdf

for a listing of self-determination curricula and components; the National Center on Secondary Education and Transition has a listing of web sites relating to self-determination for postsecondary students at:

www.ncset.org/topics/sdpse/websites.asp?topic=7

Participate and Lead IEP Meetings. At school, students can develop self-determination skills by first participating in and later by running their individualized education program (IEP) meetings (Kochhar-Bryant et al., 2009; Martin et al., 2009). Beginning in their freshman year, students should be more than just observers seated at the table at their annual IEP meeting. They should be invited to discuss what accommodations they are using, and how effective they think the accommodations are (Elksnin & Elksnin, 2009; see Step 5 for more on different types of accommodations).

Research has shown that students who run their own meetings demonstrate increased levels of self-determination, especially in the areas of goal setting and self-awareness of their transition-related skills (Martin et al., 2006). When first assuming responsibility for their meetings, students should have set steps or a plan they can follow while conducting the meeting (Martin et al., 2009). Some students will be reluctant to be in charge, so it may be appropriate to start by requiring them to provide an amount of feedback (by responding to questions about their goals, the effectiveness of their accommodations, etc.) at their first high school meeting, with the expectation and understanding that they will have to take on increasing responsibilities in subsequent meetings.

Participate in Decision Making. Of course, one of the biggest opportunities for self-determination is deciding what to do after graduation. For students who want to go to college, this goal should drive course and accommodation selection; students should take the courses they need to gain admission to college, and their accommodations should support the move toward independence (Banerjee & Brinckerhoff, 2009; Shaw, 2009). Professionals and parents working with students should show them common college entrance requirements (i.e. required courses) so that students can make an educated decision about what classes to take to make sure that they maximize their choices as they apply for college admission (see Step 6).

Giving students a voice in course selection is especially important if the IEP team is considering waiving a high school graduation requirement such as foreign language or certain math classes, as many colleges require these classes for admissions (see box, "A Word About Foreign Language Requirements"). As Madaus (2003) pointed out (and Banerjee and Brinckerhoff, 2009, reinforce), students should pursue courses that will help keep their postsecondary options open, even if they do not earn a high grade (see box, "The Professional Connection" on page 34). This means that students who want to go to college need to have the opportunity to take college prep classes in an inclusive setting, rather than a self-contained classroom, as part of the process of learning to function in the postsecondary setting. This is why it is so important for students to know something about admissions requirements as they choose their courses; they should not make such a decision without the necessary information about how it could affect their postsecondary choices. NCSET's My Future My Plan:

www.ncset.org/publications/mfmp.asp

helps students and their families plan for the post-high school transition; Landmark College has a helpful College Readiness assessment at:

www.landmark.edu/radio/documents/College-Readiness-Guide.pdf

Kochhar-Bryant (2009) recommended that transition discussions consider the kinds of skills students need to be successful at college, whether the student has these skills (and if not, which skills the student needs to develop), whether the student's accommodations are in line with those available at college, and what community supports or agencies may help prepare the student for college. These explorations incorporate the different facets of self-determination (see Figure 3-1 on page 34).

A Word About Foreign Language Requirements

Madaus (2003) counseled students, parents, and professionals not to make any assumptions about the granting of substitutions or waivers for foreign languages at college. He noted that students sometimes are kept out of these classes in high school by well-meaning parents and professionals because of the potential negative effect their grade in such classes will have on their GPA. But allowing students to avoid foreign language study while in high school level can be short-sighted. Because some colleges require that students have a certain number of years of high school foreign language in order to be considered for admission, keeping students out of foreign language in high school can limit their college choices later on. Also, some colleges require students to take foreign language in order to graduate—and they may accept a certain number of years of high school foreign language to meet this requirement. It might be better for students to take foreign language in high school, where the pace of instruction and style of teaching are typically more accessible to students with disabilities, than in college. Although students' GPA may suffer a little for it, taking a foreign language in high school helps to keep the range of options for students much wider.

Figure 3-1. Facets of Self-Determination

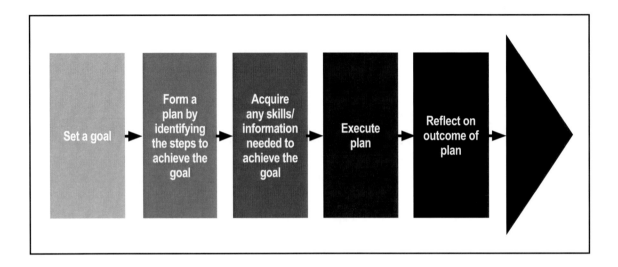

One of the best reasons to have students more involved in their IEP meetings and course selection is to make sure that their voices are heard. Because they will be in charge of asking for accommodations and asserting their rights in college, they need practice in order to develop their "voice," which is the essence of **self-advocacy**.

What is Self-Advocacy?

Self-advocacy, integral to success at the college level, is closely related to self-determination. Skinner (1998) described self-advocacy for students with disabilities as a three-pronged concept (see Figure 3-2 on page 36). Developing self-advocacy skills should be a part of students' IEPs goals and college preparatory activities.

The Professional Connection

For some students, participating in college-prep classes can be overwhelming, stressful, or damaging to their self-esteem. In such cases, students should return to the self-contained setting, and the IEP team should consider alternative postsecondary options in addition to college, where the academic and personal demands will be very challenging. Not all students, with or without disabilities, are a good match for the traditional college environment. Professionals need to be knowledgeable about other postsecondary options available to students, such as career-technical schools and job placements. They should reach out to local vocational rehabilitation offices to see what transition services are available to students, and work with local business organizations to form relationships that might help them to place students in jobs after graduation. Kochhar-Bryant and colleagues (2009) provided an overview of these choices and tips for how to help students identify the best postsecondary option.

What Things Support Student Self-Advocacy?

Knowing Their Rights. Students with disabilities must go off to college armed with the knowledge of their rights (see Step 2). It's best if this topic is covered as part of the high school's college preparatory activities (perhaps in the form of a workshop or presentation for students on IEPs and 504 plans by a knowledgeable DS staff member from a local college), so that schools ensure that all students with disabilities are introduced to this information, and they can have an opportunity to ask questions about it. But students can also find this information easily on the Internet and they should be encouraged to read this information and ask questions if they have any. The HEATH Resource Center at the National Youth Transitions Center has a brief education module for students called The Laws: What Do They Have to Do With You?

http://www.heath.gwu.edu/modules/legal-issues/

Understanding Their Disability. Throughout students' education, much of the planning and discussion happens in their absence or around them. Many students do not know much about their disability or the relevance of their accommodations to their learning needs (Foley, 2006)—yet at college, they have to be able to explain these things when they apply for services, and need to be able to speak articulately about their needs. According to research (Banerjee & Brinckerhoff, 2009; Elksnin & Elksnin, 2009), students need to:

- understand their learning profile (both impairments and strengths),

- understand how their disability impacts their functioning on academic and (if relevant) life tasks,

- know how to use their learning strengths and strategies to bypass their weaknesses,

- put a name on their disability or provide a brief explanation of it for others, and

- explain how the accommodations they want to request (see Step 5) help to mitigate the effects of their disability. The National Collaborative on Workforce and Disability's The 411 on Disability Disclosure:

  www.ncwd-youth.info/411-on-disability-disclosure

  includes several exercises for students to test their understanding of their disability.

In other words, they should know how they learn best.

Definition

Self-advocacy is being able to communicate one's needs and rights.

Figure 3-2. Components of Self-Advocacy

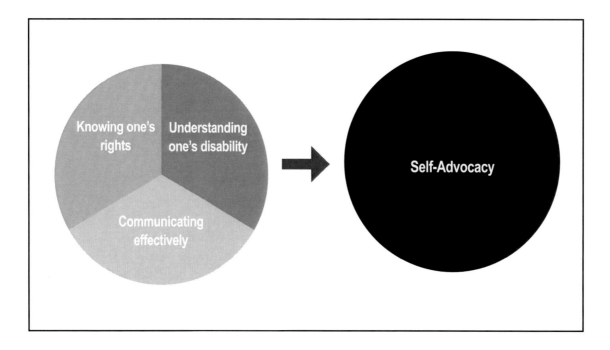

Lock & Layton (2001) modified a learning disabilities diagnostic tool for this purpose and used it to outline students' learning profiles and provide a self-advocacy plan for them to help with requesting accommodations. Such a profile can be helpful for students moving on to college to have this sort of documentation "crib sheet" of their learning style and strengths that they can use as a reference (see Step 7). Schools might use a more formal diagnostic tool such as the Learning and Study Strategies Inventory (LASSI; Weinstein, Schulte, & Palmer, 1987) as a way of questioning students about how they learn and providing them with concrete feedback about the accuracy of their perception of their own skills and what they need to work on improving in order to be ready for college. The online Learning Style Inventory at:

                    www.personal.psu.edu/bxb11/LSI/LSI.htm

provides a quick snapshot of three general categories of learning styles.

It's important for students to be engaged **metacognitively** in developing this kind of self-knowledge (Elksnin & Elksnin, 2009). A good concrete exercise to get students thinking about how they learn is to have students discuss the results of their learning style inventory with the professionals who work with them. Students' classroom teachers can provide concrete examples (e.g., graded exams or papers with comments) to show students how accurate their assessments of their own strengths and weaknesses are. Students must participate in analyzing and explaining what academic strategies work for them; after all, they will be using these strategies independently once they get to college with little external feedback on effectiveness, except for midterm and final exam grades.

Developing Communication Skills. Colleges expect students to handle all aspects of their lives on campus without assistance from their parents. Students need to be prepared to speak for themselves on a variety of fronts, and their parents need to support them in practicing effective communication skills.

Of course, for some students with disabilities, language itself is the area of difficulty. Other students do not do well interpreting social cues or following basic social conventions such as making eye contact and shaking hands. Some students with impulsivity problems interrupt others or speak without first considering what they will say or the potential consequences of their words. In the high school setting, teachers are more likely to be aware of students' communication-related difficulties, and they can typically talk to a student's case manager in the case of ineffective or inappropriate communication. However, at college, students are independent, and they are expected to communicate at a level appropriate to the setting. Banerjee and Brinckerhoff (2009) recommend that students practice self-advocacy skills in high school by being actively involved in their transition planning, contacting personnel at their target colleges with questions, and asking high school teachers for recommendation letters.

Communication itself is a multifaceted concept. Students need to understand that it involves not only what they say but how they say it, to whom, and when. This involves an understanding of how different situations will require different forms of communication, the need to be clear and, often, concise, to postpone communications at times, and the ever-important concept of tone (in other words, see box, "*communication etiquette*" on page 38-39). Some tips that can help students appropriately communicate their needs and wants include:

- ✓ Use appropriate tone of voice and body language.

- ✓ Be clear in articulating the need, problem, or request; stick to the point and avoid unnecessary details and information.

- ✓ Observe the college's formal protocols and procedures: make appointments, leave messages, and wait an appropriate amount of time for a response.

- ✓ Accommodate other people's needs and schedules.

Students can hone their communication skills by communicating with their high school teachers, counselors, and administrators; making checklists or practicing with cue cards; and role-playing with their advisors, families, and friends.

Definition

Metacognition is understanding what you know, having a sense of what you do not, and knowing how you learn best.

Communication Etiquette

Knowing what to say

Honesty is, indeed, a great policy, but it has its limits, especially when a student speaks to college staff or professors, or any authority figure. Sometimes, students with social or language-based difficulties do not understand the need for discretion. For instance, they would be ill advised to approach a professor and say, "I can't come to your office hours because it's too early in the morning, and I like to sleep in. Can I call you at home tonight to ask about my paper?" It's better, instead, if they can honestly say, "I have to be at work [or I have another class] at the time that you hold your office hours. Is there another time that would be convenient for you during which I could contact you with questions about my paper?" While they are in high school, students should be encouraged to interact with teachers, administrators, and other authority figures (e.g., coaches) in order to hone their communication skills, in a somewhat more forgiving environment.

Knowing how to say it

Rehearsal and "teachable moments" should be used while students are in high school so that they can receive concrete feedback on their communication style (e.g., "When you cross your arms, it makes you look angry or unapproachable"). Smith and colleagues (2002) suggest that students learn to use "I" language instead of "you" language when speaking to authority figures (e.g., "I experienced a problem when my professor did not give me my accommodations" rather than "He didn't do what he was supposed to do!") They should be provided with examples of clear requests or complaints and practice communicating them with an adult who can provide feedback. They should also be asked to rephrase things that they have said in different words so that it sounds less sarcastic, or to change a complaint into a question (e.g., "Is my professor allowed to tell me that I cannot use a calculator on my exam even though you approved it?).

Knowing when to say it

Students need to know that all their interactions with university personnel are governed by general etiquette rules and more formal protocols. If DS says that students have to make an appointment to see their coordinator, they should not march into the office demanding an immediate appointment. They need to know that, sometimes, they will simply have to leave a message and wait for a response. It's equally important to find the "right moment" when the communication is less formal. The time to raise personal issues (e.g. ,"I wanted to ask about my grade on the last paper") is during professors' office hours, not during class time. Communication skills include being cognizant of the needs and schedules of the people with whom one needs to communicate, as well as the needs of other students who might have more urgent issues. Does the professor need to rush out after class to start another class or catch a bus? If not, the polite approach is to say, "Professor, I have a question. Do you have a minute?"—and know that they may still have to wait for office hours anyway.

In a stressful situation (e.g., denial of accommodation or a bad grade), it's often better to wait before responding. In fact, with the exception of a situation where a professor interferes with an exam accommodation or there is a safety issue, students should know that they are always better off not expressing their thoughts immediately. Students—especially those with impulsivity problems—should seek some feedback from a friend, parent, or appropriate member of staff on what they want to say and how they plan to do it before they respond. Allowing time to collect themselves and expressing their viewpoint in a calm way can help to prevent other parties from becoming angry or upset, which can in turn keep the conversation civil and productive.

Knowing whom to contact

Students may be accustomed to having had a case manager handle their difficulties with faculty and administration in high school. At college, most DS coordinators will not run this kind of interference. Students need to know whom to approach for help for different kinds of situations (e.g., DS will not help them change dorm rooms because of a roommate problem). They should understand that it is their responsibility to communicate with professors or administrators, and that DS staff is not obligated to do this for them because they are shy or intimidated. Students should also know that it is incumbent upon them to identify the right contact person for each situation (e.g., a dean, the registrar, etc.). In the case of a complaint, an e-mail or phone call to the university president is not usually the appropriate way to handle a problem: There are procedures in place that must be followed, such as the DS grievance process.

Self-Management: Putting Self-Determination and Self-Advocacy Together

Many parents of students with disabilities are accustomed to being intimately involved in their students' lives. Although all parents of college students worry about how their children will fare there, parents of students with disabilities may be more concerned than others precisely because they know how much they, as parents, have done in making sure things go smoothly and preventing students from experiencing failure (Kochhar-Bryant, 2009; McGuire, 2009). However, this well-intentioned parenting approach holds the potential for failing to prepare students to self-advocate, especially in times of stress (Kochhar-Bryant, 2009; Smith et al., 2002). Such protectionism can be short sighted: At the postsecondary level and beyond, students need to know how to ask for what they need and capably handle conflict. The role of parents is to "prepare their child to be a responsible and capable adult" (Kochhar-Bryant, 2009, p. 157); this is why building self-determination and self-advocacy skills is so important. The HEATH Resource Center at the National Youth Transitions Center has a brief education module for parents called Parents' Guide to the Transition of Their Adult Child to College, Career, and Community at:

 www.heath.gwu.edu/modules/parents-guide-to-transition

Helping students to develop self-management skills involves such elements as making students responsible for themselves and their materials, helping them to develop the self-awareness to know when they need help, and teaching them how to ask for help appropriately (see Table 3-1 on page 41). All of these skills are involved in the homework process. According to Kochhar-Bryant (2009), students cannot develop self-awareness of their strengths and weaknesses if their parents are active participants in homework—and their teachers will not have a good sense of their true capabilities, either. Students need to get in the habit of organizing their papers and turning them in on time, perhaps using a chart to track their assignments. They also need to get in the habit of seeking help from their teachers when they do not under-stand a concept or an assignment, as it will be their responsibility to do so on their own in college.

How Can Students Develop Self-Management?

Be Responsible for Themselves. Students need to assume responsibility for daily organization tasks such as completing and turning in assignments and studying for tests—and need to experience the consequences if they do not (Kochhar-Bryant, 2009). No one at college will monitor students' daily studying and work completion, so how can they develop the skills and confidence to handle these responsibilities independently if someone does this for them? Parents can support students as they develop self-management skills by prompting them to seek support from teachers when they are struggling or when their progress reports or grades demonstrate they are having dif-ficulty. But parents should not contact teachers themselves, as this leaves the student

Table 3-1. Building Self-Advocacy

Component	Activities
Responsibility for daily organization tasks	• Completing and turning in assignments • Preparing for tests • Developing planning schedules
Responding to challenges	• Identifying areas of need • Seeking help from appropriate individual • Working out conflicts effectively
Developing postsecondary goals	• Participation in IEP meetings • Identifying appropriate accommodations • Identifying/setting postsecondary goals • Choosing appropriate high school courses

out of the process. Students need to recognize the link between missed homework, failure to seek help, or too-brief or ineffective study sessions and lower grades, and to learn study and organizational strategies.

In order to be ready to assume responsibility for themselves and their work at college, students need to learn how to function independently long before they get there. Students whose parents are too involved in their homework and studying are likely to struggle when such support disappears, as it will in college (Janiga & Costenbader, 2002; Smith et al., 2002).

Learn How to Manage Conflict. All adults need to know how to handle conflict or uncomfortable situations. To build this ability, "hold children accountable and let them experience the consequences of their actions" (Kochhar-Bryant, 2009, p. 157). Students need to have real-life experiences talking to authority figures, stating their case clearly, and handling feedback. All adults have situations where they have to ask people to fix or correct something (such as a bill), ask for help from people who do not seem inclined to assist (which can happen with a colleague), and explain their own mistakes to authority figures (such as a manager at work). While students are still in high school, parents should coach them ahead of time or attend meetings silently as a form of support if students want to talk to teachers about grades they think are unfair or meet with administrators if they get into trouble. But parents should not do the talking for students. These are learning opportunities that students need to have before college, where their parents will not be able to run interference for them. Parents can play a role in talking to students about self-advocacy and encouraging them to reflect on what did or did not work and why, but it is very important that they do not take over the advocacy role for students.

Adults can offer guidance, but high school students must handle their own conflicts as preparation to do so appropriately and independently at college (Shaw, 2009). "It is unrealistic to assume that students will be able to negotiate such problematic situations if they have not been exposed to them before or taught to work them out through problem solving" (Durlak, Rose, & Bursuck, 1994, p. 57). Students must gain the self-knowledge and communication skills they need and have the opportunity to practice these abilities before leaving for college.

The Bottom Line: Personal Skills as the Path to Success

Well-meaning professionals and parents can create an environment at home and school that does not require students to develop self-determination skills. Good intentions can lead adults to shield students from any conflict or negative outcome; this is not truly preparing them for the future. Adults cannot allow concern for students' self-esteem or the struggles they may experience to prevent them from trying things that may be difficult; struggle is a part of everyday life, even into adulthood. Adults cannot plan for students' future without including students' input in the process, so empowering students with self-advocacy skills is essential for their success.

Summary

Once students, parents, and professionals understand the amount of independence students are expected to demonstrate at college, it should become clear that they need to develop the relevant self-determination and self-advocacy skills they will need there while they are still in the structured, supportive high school environment. These skills, combined with the academic and life skills required to function at the college level, will help to promote student postsecondary success.

AIR Self-Determination Scale©

STUDENT FORM

Student's Name _____ Date_____

School Name_____ Your Grade_____

Your Date of Birth_____/_____/_____
                    Month   Date   Year

HOW TO FILL OUT THIS FORM

Please answer these questions about how you go about getting what you want or need. This may occur at school, or after school, or it could be related to your friends, your family, or a job or hobby you have.

This is not a Test.   There are no right or wrong answers. The questions will help you learn about what you do well and where you may need help.

Goal   You may not be sure what some of the words in the questions mean. For example, the word **goal** is used a lot. A **goal is something you want to get or achieve**, either now or next week or in the distant future, like when you are an adult. You can have many different kinds of goals. You could have a goal that has to do with school (like getting a good grade on a test or graduating from high school). You could have a goal of saving money to buy something (a new iPod or new sneakers), or doing better in sports (getting on the basketball team). Each person's goals are different because each person has different things that they want or need or that they are good at.

Plan   Another word that is used in some of the questions is **plan**. A **plan is the way you decide to meet your goal, or the steps you need to take in order to get what you want or need**. Like goals, you can have many different kinds of plans. An example of a plan to meet the goal of getting on the basketball team would be: to get better by shooting…more baskets at home after school, to play basketball with friends on the weekend, to listen to the coach when the team practices, and to watch the pros play basketball on TV.

The AIR Self-Determination Scale was developed by the American Institutes for Research (AIR), in collaboration with Teachers College, Columbia University, with funding from the U.S. Department of Education, Office of Special Education Programs (…), under Cooperative Agreement HO23J200005

1   *AIR* Self-Determination Scale, Student Form

HOW TO MARK YOUR ANSWERS

EXAMPLE QUESTION:

Do I check for errors after completing a project?

EXAMPLE ANSWER:

Circle the number of the answer which tells what you are most like:

(Circle **ONLY ONE** number).

1 **Never** . . . . student **never** checks for errors.

2 **Almost Never** . . . . student **almost never** checks for errors.

3 **Sometimes** . . . . student **sometimes** checks for errors.

4 **Almost Always** . . . . . . student **almost always** checks for errors.

5 **Always** . . . . student **always** checks for errors.

REMEMBER

There are NO right or wrong answers.

This will not affect your grade. So please think about each question carefully before you circle your answer.

THINGS I DO

1. I know what I need, what I like, and what I'm good at.	Never ☐ 1	Almost Never ☐ 2	Sometimes ☐ 3	Almost Always ☐ 4	Always ☐ 5
2. I set goals to get what I want or need. I think about what I am good at when I do this.	Never ☐ 1	Almost Never ☐ 2	Sometimes ☐ 3	Almost Always ☐ 4	Always ☐ 5
Things I Do – Total Items 1 + 2					
3. I figure out how to meet my goals. I make plans and decide what I should do.	Never ☐ 1	Almost Never ☐ 2	Sometimes ☐ 3	Almost Always ☐ 4	Always ☐ 5
4. I begin working on my plans to meet my goals as soon as possible.	Never ☐ 1	Almost Never ☐ 2	Sometimes ☐ 3	Almost Always ☐ 4	Always ☐ 5
Things I Do – Total Items 3 + 4					
5. I check how I'm doing when I'm working on my plan. If I need to, I ask others what they think of how I'm doing.	Never ☐ 1	Almost Never ☐ 2	Sometimes ☐ 3	Almost Always ☐ 4	Always ☐ 5
6. If my plan doesn't work, I try another one to meet my goals.	Never ☐ 1	Almost Never ☐ 2	Sometimes ☐ 3	Almost Always ☐ 4	Always ☐ 5
Things I Do – Total Items 5 + 6					

3 *AIR* Self-Determination Scale, Student Form

Reprinted with permission

HOW I FEEL

1. I feel good about what I like, what I want, and what I need to do.	Never ☐ 1	Almost Never ☐ 2	Sometimes ☐ 3	Almost Always ☐ 4	Always ☐ 5
2. I believe that I can set goals to get what I want.	Never ☐ 1	Almost Never ☐ 2	Sometimes ☐ 3	Almost Always ☐ 4	Always ☐ 5
How I Feel – Total Items 1 + 2					
3. I like to make plans to meet my goals.	Never ☐ 1	Almost Never ☐ 2	Sometimes ☐ 3	Almost Always ☐ 4	Always ☐ 5
4. I like to begin working on my plans right away.	Never ☐ 1	Almost Never ☐ 2	Sometimes ☐ 3	Almost Always ☐ 4	Always ☐ 5
How I Feel – Total Items 3 + 4					
5. I like to check on how well I'm doing in meeting my goals.	Never ☐ 1	Almost Never ☐ 2	Sometimes ☐ 3	Almost Always ☐ 4	Always ☐ 5
6. I am willing to try another way if it helps me to meet my goals.	Never ☐ 1	Almost Never ☐ 2	Sometimes ☐ 3	Almost Always ☐ 4	Always ☐ 5
How I Feel – Total Items 5 + 6					

WHAT HAPPENS AT SCHOOL

1. People at school listen to me when I talk about what I want, what I need, or what I'm good at.	Never ☐ 1	Almost Never ☐ 2	Sometimes ☐ 3	Almost Always ☐ 4	Always ☐ 5
2. People at school let me know that I can set my own goals to get what I want or need.	Never ☐ 1	Almost Never ☐ 2	Sometimes ☐ 3	Almost Always ☐ 4	Always ☐ 5
What Happens at School – Total Items 1 + 2					
3. At school, I have learned how to make plans to meet my goals and to feel good about them.	Never ☐ 1	Almost Never ☐ 2	Sometimes ☐ 3	Almost Always ☐ 4	Always ☐ 5
4. People at school encourage me to start working on my plans right away.	Never ☐ 1	Almost Never ☐ 2	Sometimes ☐ 3	Almost Always ☐ 4	Always ☐ 5
What Happens at School – Total Items 3 + 4					
5. I have someone at school who can tell me if I am meeting my goals.	Never ☐ 1	Almost Never ☐ 2	Sometimes ☐ 3	Almost Always ☐ 4	Always ☐ 5
6. People at school understand when I have to change my plan to meet my goals. They offer advice and encourage me when I'm doing this.	Never ☐ 1	Almost Never ☐ 2	Sometimes ☐ 3	Almost Always ☐ 4	Always ☐ 5
What Happens at School – Total Items 5 + 6					

5   *AIR* Self-Determination Scale, Student Form

Reprinted with permission

WHAT HAPPENS AT HOME

1. People at home listen to me when I talk about what I want, what I need, or what I'm good at.	Never ☐ 1	Almost Never ☐ 2	Sometimes ☐ 3	Almost Always ☐ 4	Always ☐ 5
2. People at home let me know that I can set my own goals to get what I want or need.	Never ☐ 1	Almost Never ☐ 2	Sometimes ☐ 3	Almost Always ☐ 4	Always ☐ 5
What Happens at Home – Total Items 1 + 2					
3. At home, I have learned how to make plans to meet my goals and to feel good about them.	Never ☐ 1	Almost Never ☐ 2	Sometimes ☐ 3	Almost Always ☐ 4	Always ☐ 5
4. People at home encourage me to start working on my plans right away.	Never ☐ 1	Almost Never ☐ 2	Sometimes ☐ 3	Almost Always ☐ 4	Always ☐ 5
What Happens at Home – Total Items 3 + 4					
5. I have someone at home who can tell me if I am meeting my goals.	Never ☐ 1	Almost Never ☐ 2	Sometimes ☐ 3	Almost Always ☐ 4	Always ☐ 5
6. People at home understand when I have to change my plan to meet my goals. They offer advice and encourage me when I'm doing this.	Never ☐ 1	Almost Never ☐ 2	Sometimes ☐ 3	Almost Always ☐ 4	Always ☐ 5
What Happens at Home – Total Items 5 + 6					

PLEASE WRITE YOUR ANWERS TO THE FOLLOWING QUESTIONS...

Give an example of a goal you are working on.

_____

_____

_____

_____

What are you doing to reach this goal?

_____

_____

_____

_____

How well are you doing in reaching this goal?

_____

_____

_____

_____

THANK YOU!

7   *AIR* Self-Determination Scale, Student Form

Reprinted with permission

The AIR Self-Determination Profile Student Form

	Thinks	Do	Adjust		Thinks	Do	Adjust
Items	1-2	3-4	5-6	Items	1-2	3-4	5-6
10				10			
9				9			
8				8			
7				7			
6				6			
5				5			
4				4			
3				3			
2				2			
1				1			
0				0			

Total ____ ____ ____   Total ____ ____ ____

Things I Do   How I Feel

	Thinks	Do	Adjust		Thinks	Do	Adjust
Items	1-2	3-4	5-6	Items	1-2	3-4	5-6
10				10			
9				9			
8				8			
7				7			
6				6			
5				5			
4				4			
3				3			
2				2			
1				1			
0				0			

Total ____ ____ ____   Total ____ ____ ____

What Happens at School   What Happens at Home

120 110 100 90 80 70 60 50 40 30 20 10 0

100% 90% 80% 70% 60% 50% 40% 30% 20% 10%

Capacity

+

Opportunity

=

Level of Self-Determination (Write sum in box and mark in column)

Name _____ Date
_____

8 *AIR* Self-Determination Scale, Student Form

Reprinted with permission

Step 4

Develop College Survival Skills

The adjustment to the postsecondary environment can be difficult for many students, with or without disabilities. The lack of structure and supervision, the fact that classes meet less frequently, and other lifestyle and learning environment changes require many freshmen to change the way they do things. It is important for students with disabilities to be aware of the challenges they will face in this new environment, and be prepared to meet them. The academic, fundamental, technology, and independent living skills discussed in this chapter are truly "survival" skills and are important for all students who aspire to go to college—regardless of whether or not they have a disability.

Step 4

Develop College Survival Skills

The adjustment to the postsecondary environment can be difficult for many students, with or without disabilities. The lack of structure and supervision, the fact that classes meet less frequently, and other lifestyle and learning environment changes require many freshmen to change the way they do things. It is important for students with disabilities to be aware of the challenges they will face in this new environment, and to be prepared to meet them. The academic, technology, and independent living skills discussed in this chapter are truly "survival" skills and are important for all students who aspire to go to college—regardless of whether or not they have a disability.

It is critical to make sure that students arrive at college with the academic skills they will need to be successful, as they will be expected to read and write with a certain level of sophistication, and certain accommodations (see Step 5) may not be available to them. Development of these skills should be a natural part of students' work in high school, not necessarily something that needs to be taught outside the context of the classroom. High school individualized education program (IEP) teams should make sure that students who want to go to college take college prep classes and work to a level appropriate in those classes so that they have the required credits they need to get in to college and are prepared for the kind of work they will have to do in college (Banerjee & Brinckerhoff, 2009; Elksnin & Elksnin, 2009). Although IEP team members might be concerned about students' grades being affected by taking challenging college preparatory classes, they must keep in mind that working at the college prep level is crucial in helping students develop the academic skills they need to be successful at college (Banerjee & Brinckerhoff, 2009).

High school students who are making decent grades may not see a reason to improve or add to their academic or study skills. This is why it is important to educate them about the challenges that the college environment may pose, and to support them in developing the academic, fundamental, technology, and independent living skills they will need to meet these challenges.

How College Differs From High School

Academic Expectations

Academic expectations at college can be very different from those in high school. Students are expected to think and write at a higher level than they may have done before, and they have to integrate information from a variety of sources (Brinckerhoff,

1996). For instance, rather than listing the causes of the American Revolution on an exam, it's more likely that students will need to explain how political and economic forces led to the revolt.

Classes

Classes at college typically meet only two or three times a week, which means that students may miss the reinforcement of concepts that occurs when classes meet every day. Some long seminars meet only once a week, so if students are sick on the day a class meets, they may miss a lot of information. Classes may be several hours apart in a given day (students may have a 10:00 a.m. class and not have another class until 2:00 p.m.), which means students with distractibility problems may find it challenging to get to classes after they have transitioned to lunch or another activity away from the classroom buildings.

In addition to the overall class schedule, the format of classes may be very challenging. There are still many professors who hold to the standard lecture format (even in a 3-hour class), which can be troublesome for students with all kinds of learning problems (as well as those without). Long lectures can be exhausting for students with attention, listening, or language-based disorders, especially as some professors simply talk without providing any supporting visual materials to supplement their lectures (see box, "A Word About Notetaking").

Exams

The importance placed on exams at college can be particularly challenging for some students with disabilities. At college, the big midterm and final exams are often the only opportunities for students to show what they have learned; there may be no assignments or projects students can complete in order to boost their grades. For students who are not good test-takers (and for those with bad time management skills who leave studying to the last minute), this can make exams an even greater anxiety-provoking experience.

A Word About Notetaking

Notetaking is an essential skill. In college, students need to adjust to the pace of lecturing and the fact that, in some classes, there are no accompanying visuals. Although some professors use whiteboards or PowerPoint presentations (and make copies of these or copies of their own notes available on the Internet), others simply talk for 2 or 3 hours. Students must find ways to capture information. Although there are helpful technology products for recording everything that is said during a class (see Step 5), students still need to learn methods for getting notes down and arranging them in a format that makes sense to them.

Exam format is typically dictated by the size and nature of the class. Large introductory-level classes may have extensive multiple-choice exams where answers are recorded on Scantron sheets. As students move into more specialized classes for their major, they may take "blue book" exams, where they have to write essays in response to exam questions and fill as many books as they can in the allotted time. At some colleges, testing is conducted on computers. Students should be aware of all of the different types of exams they can expect to encounter at college.

Studying

Students excited about the limited number of hours they'll spend in class in college (12–15 hours a week in college vs. 30–35 hours a week in high school) should recognize that the reason for this change is that they are expected to do a lot of learning on their own, through readings and assignments (see box, "College Survival: Managing the Workload" on page 55). Brinckerhoff (1996, p. 119) offers this rule of thumb

---

$$\frac{\text{2 hours of studying x 1 hour of class x 3-4 class hours per day}}{= \text{6-8 hours of studying per day}}$$

This is why it is crucial for students to:

- ✓ Develop a regular study schedule while they are in high school and get a sense of their prime studying time and environment (Hong, Ivy, Gonzalez, & Ehrensberger, 2007; Skinner & Lindstrom, 2003).

- ✓ Develop independent time management skills so that they do not get too far behind or, even better, get ahead on readings and assignments (Hong et al., 2007; Skinner & Lindstrom, 2003).

- ✓ Understand the connection between studying, being on top of readings and assignments, paying attention to lectures, and success in classes (Hong et al., 2007)

One aspect of college that frustrates some students with disabilities is that they realize for the first time how much more time they need to study than their peers do (Brinckerhoff, 1996; Rath & Royer, 2002). But students should take some comfort in the idea that the work ethic they develop in studying effectively will carry over to the rest of their adult lives, and will be an asset to them in the future (see box, "A Word About Study Groups" on page 56).

College Survival: Managing the Workload

Seek Assistance. Colleges expect students to manage their time well enough to complete out-of-class assignments and exams by the given deadline. Although the college tutoring or learning center can help students to plan their assignments, set up progressive deadlines, organize their notes, and edit their drafts, it is up to students to access this assistance. Students might consider starting college with a reduced course load (see Step 5) so that they can get used to managing deadlines while taking only a few classes at a time. Students who have to work or have other obligations that interfere with their study time also should consider asking for a reduced course load.

Seek a Balanced Load. Students should also try to balance their course load to the extent that they are able. For instance, students with reading difficulties should avoid registering for several courses with heavy reading loads (e.g., history classes) during the same semester; it helps to research the courses students plan to take before making their choices. Students also can ask the DS staff if they there are other students with disabilities to whom they can speak to get a sense of what kinds of workloads certain professors assign. (Students who visit online sites such as Rate My Professors:

www.ratemyprofessors.com/

should assess the information provided critically, understanding that some students post negative reviews for personal reasons, because they didn't do well in the class, or because the class was more difficult than they anticipated.)

Seek Alternatives. Students might also consider taking required courses (i.e., classes required by the college's distribution requirements or those needed to complete a degree in their major) that present real challenges for them during a winter or summer session. Registering for just a single course during one of these periods will give them the time and energy to focus on that class. Alternatively, students might be able to take these difficult courses at their local community college. Community colleges are a greatly undervalued resource for students with disabilities. Professors at these schools are accustomed to working with students with disabilities, and they typically know how to pace challenging classes to support students' acquisition of the material. Before registering for such a class, though, students should check with their college to make sure that the community college credits will transfer.

Reading Assignments

The reading load in college is much greater than it is in high school. Reading assignments generally fall into three categories:

- those assigned ahead of when they will be discussed in class so that students will come into class with some background in what will be discussed,

- those chosen to enhance or extend topics discussed in class, and

- those given to cover information professors want students to know but don't have time to discuss in class.

Students are responsible for the content of assigned readings when taking their exams, even if professors never discussed these in class. Life at college will be much easier for students if, for example, they are already accustomed to using software and other tools (see Step 5) to help them get through their piles of reading. Students need to have a realistic sense of how long it takes them to read a certain number of pages—and whether they will have to reread for retention—so that they can plan their study time accordingly.

The Teaching Staff

Professors. Although students will certainly find helpful professors at college, they need to know that access to them will be much more limited than it was in high school (Hong et al, 2007; Sitlington, 2003). Most professors are on campus only 2 or 3 days a week, and they may adhere to their office hours quite rigidly—and during office hours, there may be a line of other students also waiting to see them (see box, "A Word About Office Hours" on page 57). Students who really need to see their professors should plan to be at the office for the whole time that the professor is seeing students, in case they have to wait until the professor has seen students who arrived before them.

A Word About Study Groups

The average student does not want to spend any "extra" time studying. For students with disabilities—who may already be spending more time studying than their peers or who are sensitive about their learning issues—the idea of a study group may be unappealing. However, reviewing notes with peers can be a great way to check comprehension. Students might also discover from their peers a new way of taking notes or preparing for exams. Such collaborative efforts can carry social benefits and may give students a sense of how their skills measure up. They may even learn that they have the best study strategies in the group, if they have been working on these before college.

Even when they are eager to help, most professors have little training or experience in working with students with disabilities (Hong et al., 2007). Some may even harbor negative ideas about students with learning disabilities and other kinds of invisible disabilities and their accommodations. Research shows that some professors worry that accommodations result in lowered academic standards for their courses (Lock & Layton, 2001). Some professors believe that students who use disability accommodations are lazy and underqualified for college, and that their accommodations give them an academic advantage (Lock & Layton, 2001). Some even think that they do not have to allow accommodations (Lock & Layton, 2001); this is why it is very important for students to understand their rights and to know, before the semester starts, how (and when) to approach their professors (see box, "How to Talk to Professors—and When" on pages 58-59), and how to handle situations where professors try prevent them from using their accommodations, even though this is unlikely to happen (see Step 2 for more on students' rights).

Teaching Assistants (TAs). TAs can sometimes be students' best resource for help. Because they are graduate students, TAs tend to be on campus more often than professors. Some may offer weekly study groups that review content covered in class, and they may even hold special reviews before exams. Some may be aspiring professors who are especially eager to be helpful to students, and who may offer more assistance than professors can because of other commitments.

Technology

Students need to be aware of the ways that technology will be used in various parts of their education, and be comfortable using it. Colleges have eliminated quite a bit of paper from their processes; communication to students typically happens through e-mails and, in case of emergency, text alerts. Registration is online during certain assigned periods. Even the submission of assignments may be done electronically.

A Word About Office Hours

The best way to talk with a professor or ask individual questions is during office hours. If students have classes or work during professors' office hours, they shouldn't give up: They can approach professors after class or through e-mail, explain the legitimate reason why they cannot attend the regular office hours, and ask whether there is another way to communicate or meet. Students shouldn't e-mail professors repeatedly, though, and should be patient in waiting for a response; they have to demonstrate realistic expectations by using e-mail sparingly and appropriately. They should not attempt to circumvent office hours for anything but legitimate reasons (i.e., work or classes). If unsure what a professor's office hours are, students should check the syllabus, or call department and ask the secretary about the procedure for getting an appointment.

Surviving in the College Environment

Students at college are expected to read and write with a certain level of sophistication, and these expectations are held for all college students, even those with disabilities. They also need to be able to manage their time and assignments, and have strategies to help them compensate for their disability. In addition, students need to be well versed in the range of technology supports available to assist them and be able to handle independent living. Developing these "College Survival Skills" (see Figure 4-1 on page 60), along with the personal skills discussed in Step 3, helps to ensure success at the postsecondary level.

How to Talk to Professors—and When

Whether to disclose more than the information in their letter of accommodation (LOA; see Step 2) challenges students to put their self-determination and self-advocacy skills (see Step 3) to work. Students who are comfortable enough to do this should be applauded—but they may benefit from some pointers to make the conversation as productive as possible.

1. Although the LOA should be handed over to professors as soon as possible (and according to DS recommendations), students might find it helpful not to disclose more information than the LOA contains until they have attended a class or two. By doing this, they will get a sense of the professor's personality and any possible biases.

2. If they decide to self-disclose, students should choose the appropriate moment—generally, during office hours. Buttonholing a professor at the beginning or end of class is generally not the right time. Before class, professors are often very focused on what they plan to do during that class, and many are busy setting up and attending to "housekeeping" (e.g., handing out papers, taking attendance, etc.). At the end of class, some may have to rush across campus for their next class, and others may have other students waiting to ask questions. Neither of these scenarios allows the time, attention, and privacy required for this important discussion. More important, it may be inconvenient timing for the professor.

3. It is important that students prepare what they want to say. They need to be able to articulate their diagnosis simply and explain why the accommodations for which they have been approved help them to compete at the same level as their peers (see Step 6's Accommodation Request Preparation Form for some questions to help formulate the conversation points). Although professors may be impressed by a student's perseverance and prior hard work, what they really want to know is what they need to do for this student now, not what was done in the past. Students should be prepared to say what they need to in a concise and persuasive way and understand that, when it comes to talking, sometimes less is more.

Academic Skills

Writing Skills

In college, students are expected to write essays that are more sophisticated and require more analysis. Students who have difficulty figuring out what to say need to learn scaffolding techniques to help them organize their ideas. Some students find it more useful to use graphic organizers, concept maps, or idea maps than to try to compose an outline. Whatever method they decide works best for them, it is important that students know how to organize and develop their ideas when writing papers in college.

4. Students should avoid attempting to "convert" professors who have negative attitudes about students with disabilities; attempting to do so may create an adversarial relationship. Part of becoming an adult is accepting the idea that you cannot always change people's minds through persuasion. And, even if a professor has negative ideas about students with disabilities, he still cannot deny a student approved accommodations, so there is no need to try to make him think differently. In such cases, a businesslike approach is really the best one to use.

5. Students who want to ask professors for additional accommodations that go beyond those for which they have been approved should know that there may be a risk in doing so. Although at some colleges, the DS office wants the conversation about accommodations to happen between students and professors with little guidance, at other schools DS and professors alike may view such requests as inappropriate attempts to circumvent the system. Trying to get additional accommodations by going directly to professors (especially if these accommodations have been denied by DS) may establish an unpleasant dynamic between students and the professionals with whom they work. Before making additional requests, students should be sure of the college's philosophy, and be very careful about attempting to work outside the system if the college wants accommodations to be granted only through DS.

    If professors ask what additional adjustments might be helpful, students are certainly welcome to respond. But if professors do not offer an opportunity to ask for more, students should be careful about requesting additional accommodations that have not been approved through the proper channels, unless the DS philosophy is one where students are encouraged to go directly to their professors. Again, students should gauge professors' receptiveness before making additional requests.

Figure 4-1. College Survival Skills

Others may find it helpful to utilize speech-to-text software or apps (e.g. Dragon) as a way of simply getting their ideas down so that they can later go back and develop them. Inspiration:

                                    www.inspiration.com/inspiration

is perhaps the best-known software for concept mapping; the program also enables the user to convert the graphic organizer to outline format. Bubble.us and Text 2 Mind Map:

                                        www.text2mindmap.com

offer free online concept mapping programs.

College-bound students also need experience in the nuts and bolts of writing papers, such as doing research and properly citing sources. Students should know how to find reliable sources using library databases and the Internet without losing hours to fruitless searches. They also need to be able to accurately cite and source rephrased information to avoid inadvertent plagiarism and should get in the habit of taking down all of information they will need for later use in a bibliography.

                                        www.Turnitin.com

A system many high schools and colleges use to check student work for inadvertent or purposeful plagiarism also offers WriteCheck; students can submit a certain number of revisions of a paper to check for themselves whether or not they have unwittingly plagiarized sources.

Reading

Students with and without disabilities can be overwhelmed by the amount of reading required in college, and many are not strategic when trying to get through numerous chapters of text. For students with reading, memory, and language problems, college-level reading can be a real challenge. Beginning early in high school, students need to learn strategies for reading comprehension (e.g., survey/question/read/recite [SQ3R], highlighting, notetaking, using technology). This training should provide them with the confidence and tools to approach different types of readings in a way that suits them and facilitates their studying later.

College **syllabi** provide only a vague overview of course requirements for the entirety of the class; students often start the semester with a stack of textbooks and are never asked to "prove" that they have read anything—until that midterm exam. Rather than reading and digesting 350 pages in 3 days, college students need to be able to plan for long-term reading assignments. While still in high school, students should learn to develop a reading schedule to keep up with a summer or long-term reading assignments as a part of their preparation for college reading loads.

Notetaking

While they are still in high school, students should practice with different kinds of note formats (e.g., Cornell notes, webs) and decide what works best for them. Some students like linear, word-filled notes, while others prefer short phrases arranged visually to show the relationships between ideas, and still others may draw a graphic organizer. This is why self-knowledge of learning style is so important. The Cornell notetaking system is explained at:

www.sc.sas.cornell.edu/Sidebars/Study_Skills_Resources/cornellsystem.pdf

Many students think that they need to take down every word that is said in a class in its entirety. Instead, they should learn to develop their own shorthand (dropping

---

Definition

A **syllabus** is a list or calendar given out in college classes that contains weekly assignments and readings, exam dates, and paper deadlines. Students will have one for each different class, either on paper or electronically—but students should remember that it may not always be accurate or may change as the semester progresses.

small words and making up abbreviations for words commonly used in their classes) so that they can increase their notetaking speed. Students are already doing this when they text friends; they just need to think about applying this technique to their classes. They should develop this system while they are in high school so that they are ready to face the challenge of fast-moving college lectures.

Study Strategies and Metacognition—An Important Combination

To most high school students (with or without disabilities), studying is something you do a night or two before a test. But much of a college student's time is expected to involve independent studying—reading, taking notes, and digesting information (Brinckerhoff, 1996; Hong et al., 2007). It may be difficult for students to know, even when they are keeping up with assignments, whether or not they really understand what their professors expect them of them (Brinckerhoff, 1996; see box, "College Survival: Knowing When to Ask for Help"). Metacognition is a skill that students must develop before college (Elksnin & Elksnin, 2009; Skinner & Lindstrom, 2003); if they are too reliant upon outside sources for feedback (e.g., tests and teacher comments), they will not develop the intrinsic skills they will need at college to check their comprehension.

And they should know how they study best. Some students do better going to the library for several hours at a time, whereas others need a break every hour or can only do 2 hours at a time before they need a longer break. Students must have this level of self-knowledge before they get to college so that they can organize themselves

College Survival: Knowing When to Seek Help

At college, students may be surprised by how little feedback they get on how they are doing in class. The expectation, however, is that students are in charge of their own learning and are monitoring their own progress. At most colleges, a tutoring or academic support center can help students figure out whether they are up to date with work and check their understanding—but students have to seek out this assistance. Professors do not give out progress reports; their only assessments of students' progress will be their responses to papers and exams.

Students who are keeping up with the readings yet do not understand them, or are struggling with the work itself, must seek help, either by meeting with professors during office hours or making an appointment at the campus tutoring center. It is not the responsibility of professors in whose classes students may be struggling (or even failing) to suggest to them that they get help. Nor is it the responsibility of academic advisors, who typically only see students once a semester to help them choose their classes. Although a student's DS coordinator might help make the first appointment for tutoring or arrange for a special orientation to the writing lab, DS personnel are not responsible for encouraging students to go for tutoring, to make appointments for them, or to check up on them to see whether they have gone for help.

and keep up with expectations in the vast amount of unstructured time that is a college student's schedule.

While they are still in high school, students should learn a variety of study strategies, such as

- Rewriting or making idea maps of lecture notes and notes from readings, summarizing or paraphrasing readings and class notes, and finding other ways to make sure that they understand the topics and can explain them clearly (Brinckerhoff, 1996).

- Developing mnemonics that are effective for them (rather than using ones someone else provides that don't make sense to them) and using other memorization techniques (Skinner & Lindstrom, 2003).

- Reviewing notes repeatedly over the course of the semester to reduce study time (and anxiety) when it comes time for the exam and to better ensure that the information is cemented in memory.

- Using chapter questions or working with a classmate to review information discussed in class and readings to make sure it has been mastered.

Although students may see such exercises as time consuming, they should understand that these exercises provide the content review they are used to via nightly high school homework assignments. Using these techniques will provide a solid foundation for success when students get to college.

Fundamental Skills

Developing academic skills is important so that students can take on the challenges of the college environment. But they also need a solid foundation in certain fundamental skills that help make studying easier and more effective.

Organization and Time Management

These skills are the glue that holds other study and academic skills together. Students need to be able to manage their time and organize their materials (Skinner & Lindstrom, 2003) in order to put their other skills to work.

While they are in high school, students may have organization imposed on them by teachers who do notebook checks or by parents or tutors who make them attend to their papers on a regular basis. Their schedule also provides structure: they go to classes all day, then have the after-school hours in which to study. Since these scaffolds are not present when students move to college, they have to have systems in place with which they are comfortable so that they are ready for success.

Students should have one central planning tool where they record assignment deadlines and other dates they need to remember. They need to know, before they get to college, whether they function better with a paper or electronic organizer. They should know which format or layout works better, too. For instance, some students with working memory problems may prefer a planner that shows them a month at a time, whereas students with visual perceptual problems may benefit from seeing only one day at a time. Any planner should have plenty of space to list appointments, assignments, school-related paperwork (e.g., course registration) deadlines, and test dates. And there should be a place to keep a to-do list (Skinner & Lindstrom, 2003).

In college, students are responsible for keeping their materials organized, too. Unlike high school, where teachers often dictate how tests, papers, notes, and other class papers should be maintained, in college this is another responsibility of students. Some students do better with one big binder that contains individual folders for every class. Others prefer separate notebooks and like to use color-coding (e.g., having a blue binder for Economics and putting all deadlines for that class in the calendar in blue). Some may use a hybrid system. Whatever they choose to do, it should make sense to them, and the best way to make sure of this is to try out a system in high school that makes them comfortable so that they can utilize it at college.

The amount of free time outside of classes can be overwhelming to students, especially if they are accustomed to having a full schedule. As a way of coping, students should consider their study time and time at their school's help centers as regular appointments in their schedule, just like classes (Skinner & Lindstrom, 2003). This way, they will keep up with what they have to do.

Compensatory Strategies

Students need to learn compensatory techniques specific to their disability (Madaus, 2009) to help them bypass or compensate for academic weaknesses. These range from technology supports, cognitive strategies, and creating mnemonics to time management skills, depending upon the individual student's needs. Although some students develop these on their own, often without realizing they're doing it (especially students who aren't identified as having an attention disorder or a learning disability until later in their education), many students do not. While they are in high school, special education teachers need to teach students strategies that match with their profile of strengths and weaknesses, and they should be explicit about explaining how these strategies are appropriate for students based on their profile, as this will help to develop students' self-knowledge.

Technology Skills

Becoming familiar with technologies that make academic work easier is certainly to students' advantage. But as Banerjee (2009) points out, students also need to make sure that they are fluent in everyday computer competencies.

Using Basic Word Processing Tools, Presentation Programs, and Databases

In addition to spell and grammar check, they should know how to insert footnotes, a header, or a text box. For presentations, they will need familiarity with programs such as PowerPoint and may need to know how to insert video and animation into their projects (Banerjee, 2009). In some areas of study, students need to know how to build a database. Again, they are likely already using these skills for high school assignments. If they do not need to perform these functions in order to complete their assignments for high school, they should practice on their own with a made-up assignment over the summer, or take a class offered by their library or county adult education program.

Organizing Files and Documents on the Computer

During their high school years, students should get in the habit of creating folders on their computer for each class they take and storing their assignments and notes in them to help keep them organized and easy to locate. Students may find that their computer's software offers other helpful tools such as calendars and virtual "sticky notes" that they can use to keep track of deadlines.

Using the Internet

Students should know how to generate relevant topic words to put into a search engine or database search feature and then how to use the advanced features of these programs to narrow down their results. Once they get their results, they need to be able to figure out what kinds of sources they have found and how to cite them in their papers. They should know how to upload papers to the Internet, and how to download and save files from e-mails and online sources to a folder on their desktop (rather than to a temporary Internet file, which can be hard to find). Students who struggle with distractions should consider investing in Freedom:

www.macfreedom.com/

an Internet blocking program that will prevent them from spending too much time surfing the web instead of studying.

Backing up Work

Although technology makes many aspects of students' academic work easier, it can be a huge source of stress when it malfunctions, and professors may not accept a crashed hard drive as an excuse for late work. Students should practice backing up and recovering their work, and get in the habit of maintaining some kind of copy (paper or electronic) every time they work on a draft. (Students who do not want to print copies of their drafts after each work session because of a concern for the environment can either e-mail themselves a copy of their draft after every work session or use a free online document repository such as Google Docs or Microsoft Office Live. This way, they will have something to show to professors in case of a computer disaster.)

Assistive Technology

In the college environment, students with disabilities are expected to keep up with their classmates and will have to do a lot of studying and preparation without the supports they may have relied on in the past, such as parents or special education teachers. This can be daunting to students, but assistive technology might give them the tools they need to manage their work in the postsecondary world (Banerjee, 2009; Marshak, Van Wieren, Ferrell, Swiss, & Dugan, 2010; Shaw, 2009). Experimenting with technology in high school also will help students to decide what kind of technological accommodations to request (see Table 5-2, p. 110), as colleges might not offer such help to them unless they ask for it (Banerjee, 2009). And because colleges often use technology instead of human help in providing accommodations (e.g., offering text-to-speech software instead of a human reader), it's a good idea for students to become familiar with these technologies before they go to college.

When learning to use software or equipment, students should remember that the particular product they are using (e.g., Read & Write GOLD) may not be the one available at college, and that colleges are not required to buy students' preferred programs for use on exams (Banerjee, 2009). Even in this type of situation, experience in using any kind of technology will likely reduce students' learning curve for whatever program their college utilizes (Banerjee, 2009). When researching software students should investigate whether several of the programs they want to use are compatible with each other, or try to find one program that combines all of the features they hope to use. For example, while still in high school, students might explore the following technology:

- Working with audio books from Learning Ally (www.learningally. com, formerly Recording for the Blind & Dyslexic [RFB&D]).

- How text-to-speech programs and screen readers work.

- Using speech-to-text programs for dictating and mapping software for organizing ideas for papers.

- Using a handheld spell or grammar checker when writing essays; exploring computer-based spellcheck features and spelling software.

- Using a digital recorder while taking notes as a way of catching missed information (noting counter number when they think they might have missed something and scanning to that point when filling in missed notes later).

Practicing with such technology while they're in high school will mean that students will need less time to learn to use these programs and devices in college, which can be a big help while they work to keep up with academic demands.

Students should be aware that many colleges use course management systems where students register for classes, check assignment deadlines, upload completed work, and perform other functions associated with classes, such as participating in real-time online discussions (Banerjee, 2009). Although students may not get a chance to practice using these systems before they go to college, they should at least be aware that they exist. After students get their acceptances and decide where they will enroll, they can call their school to ask what course management software they use so that they can look it up on the Internet and at least familiarize themselves with the program and what it does. Some schools may provide training on these systems during freshman orientation.

Life Skills

All students at college face new challenges and learn new skills. Because academic demands may be a big source of stress, students with disabilities should start practicing essential "life skills" before they leave home, so that the everyday aspects of their independent lives do not add additional stress. If they do not already do this, they should:

- Start a laundry routine, making sure they have enough essentials (i.e., underwear and socks) to last a week.

- Have a checkbook and be responsible for balancing it.

- Have a credit card for essentials and be responsible for paying the bill on time.

- Get in the habit of using planners or other organizing methods (e.g., the calendar on their cell phone) to manage real-life commitments like doctors appointments.

- Get in the habit of cleaning out and attending to important e-mails at least once a week, not leaving anything in their in-box for longer than a few days.

- Know basic phone and conversational skills (e.g., introducing themselves before asking to whom they are speaking on the phone, shaking hands firmly while making eye contact, how to ask someone's name if they have forgotten it).

These are the kinds of "soft" skills that schools do not teach but parents can help students to develop through a combination of direct instruction and feedback when they utilize these skills in real-life situations. The best thing that parents can do is to help students develop independent living skills while they are still at home.

Dorm Life and Roommates

Dorm living can be a real impediment to studying and an invitation to waste time. Students who prefer to study in a quiet environment may have to go to the library, which is only open during certain hours. Those who need to read aloud as a comprehension aid may be asked by their roommates to go elsewhere to do this. Students with impulsivity and time management problems may find the social aspects of dorm life, where there always seems to be someone looking to socialize, a real challenge to self-discipline. Students should know that the dormitory resident directors' and advisors' job is simply to oversee the students in a general way, not to take the place of parents by forcing students to lock their friends out of their rooms and study, or to settle every roommate squabble. All freshmen have to learn how make their living situation work (even if it means leaving their room to study at times) and exercise self-discipline in the absence of an enforcer to make them turn away from distractions and work on their assignments.

Social Activities

All new college students have to learn to navigate social activities and events; some students with disabilities will find it more difficult to establish a balance. At many schools, binge drinking continues to be a problem for all kinds of students, and it is an activity that goes on all week long. Students with impulsivity problems may find it difficult to restrict their social activities to the weekends and to know when to stop drinking. Students on certain medications should not drink because it can cause dangerous interactions with their prescriptions. Students who go off of their medication when they get to college (the better to "blend in," they typically say) can end up self-medicating with alcohol and drugs. Students with autism spectrum disorders or anxiety problems may drink to excess as a way to gain approval or to relax enough to go out. Again, although these pitfalls have to be navigated by all college freshmen, students with certain disabilities may find resisting these social pressures even more difficult.

Students transitioning to college understandably focus on the academic challenges that they will encounter, and they may think of the freedoms and social aspects of colleges as all positive. It can be helpful to alert students to the downside of some of their freedoms that so that they are aware of them and have a chance to seek some advice on how to cope with them (see box, "A Word About Campus Tours" on page 69).

Summary

Because the elementary and secondary school special education system tends to put adults in charge of many facets of students' education, the emphasis is not always on helping students to do things for themselves. It is imperative that professionals, parents, and students themselves remember the importance of students' developing the skills they will need to manage independently when they get to college. If students develop a strong foundation in academic, study, and self-management skills, they will be miles ahead of most of their classmates, many of whom will find that the new academic environment forces them to work harder than they had to in high school. From this solid base, students can pursue the accommodations that will help to level the playing field for them at college and allow them to perform to the best of their ability.

A Word About Campus Tours

Campus tours can give students a sense of a college's campus and the general living environment. But some students want to know more about a school; they may have a special interest in knowing what the environment is like for students with disabilities. During their college search, students with such questions should contact DS at the colleges they are considering attending and ask if DS can connect them—by phone or e-mail—with a student who would be willing to speak with them about their experiences in the dorms and classes. This will give students the opportunity to ask any specific questions they have that can really only be answered by another student.

Step 5

Understand College Accommodations

Accommodations are what the student needs to be able to access the curriculum. But how do students establish exactly which accommodations to request? Are some more likely to be approved than others? What alternatives do students have to accommodations they've used in high school? Students with disabilities need to understand how to apply for accommodations and the possible range of supports available, and to be prepared to assume responsibility for the process.

Step 5

Understand College Accommodations

As discussed in Step 1, federal law requires colleges to provide "reasonable" accommodations for students with disabilities. But two factors can affect whether or not colleges make certain accommodations available to students: exceptions in the law regarding what is not "reasonable" and expectations for students' independent functioning in the college setting. This is why the conversation about what accommodations students might utilize in college should begin as early as the eighth grade, as individualized education programs (IEPs) and Section 504 plans are being written for students' freshman year (Banerjee & Brinckerhoff, 2009). Academic planning and accommodations should further the long-term goal of assisting students in developing and using effective study techniques and strategies that help them to bypass their learning difficulties—and students' accommodations and instruction should reflect this goal.

Federal law does not provide a list of accommodations that schools must make. Instead, Section 504 of the Rehabilitation Law of 1973 says that

> Auxiliary aids may include taped texts, interpreters or other effective methods of making orally delivered materials available to students with hearing impairments, readers in libraries for students with visual impairments, classroom equipment adapted for use by students with manual impairments, and other similar services and actions. (34 C.F.R. § 104.44[d][2])

Although this lists a few suggestions, it is not a mandate for providing these particular adjustments for each student with the listed impairment. Obviously, it is also not an exhaustive list that covers all sorts of disabilities; colleges can—and some do—go far beyond these adjustments.

Most students who utilize somewhat minimal accommodations (e.g., extended time or handheld spellchecker for exams) will likely find their desired accommodations available to them at college. Those whose accommodations are very supportive (e.g., students whose teachers provide them with a prepared study guide before tests) may find that, due to the expectations and exceptions previously mentioned, their requested accommodations are not available. As discussed, any requests that students make will be reviewed with several considerations in mind.

Students with "mild" conditions also should be aware that, at some schools, they might not qualify for an accommodation (McGuire, 2009). The laws governing equal access to postsecondary education state that a *handicap* "substantially limits one or more major life activities" (42 U.S.C. § 12102), but do not provide concrete requirements for determining how substantial the limitation has to be (e.g., a student whose scores on all math measures fall below the 25th percentile). So, scores that qualify students for services at College A may find that College B does not find them sufficiently low to qualify as "substantially limited."

What Do Colleges Consider When Reviewing Accommodations Requests?

Do the Requested Accommodations Meet the Student's Specific Needs?

Disability Services (DS) offices expect students to request accommodations that are supported by evidence from **psychoeducational testing** or other forms of documentation (meaning, relevant to the student's specific weaknesses; see Step 7). Colleges do not want to see what appears to be a standard, generic list of adjustments that seems unrelated to a student's specific documented weaknesses; instead, they want to see a rationale for each recommended accommodation that is supported by documentation. Colleges must treat students with disabilities as individuals. There is not a standard set of accommodations granted for each category of disability, so they expect the documentation to explain why each recommended accommodation is necessary to give the student access to the curriculum and the rest of the college's programs.

Some colleges may be very particular about whether students' psychoeducational testing scores qualify for (or exclude them from) accommodation. For instance, some colleges may declare that a particular level of discrepancy is required between abilities (e.g., 1.5 standard deviations between students' verbal IQ and reading skills) in order to demonstrate the presence of a disability. Other schools may say that there has to be a weakness demonstrated on all of the tests of the area of purported weakness (e.g., reading). In a recent study, 49% of the colleges surveyed indicated that they required students' scores to show some discrepancy in order to qualify them for services, though requirements for how much variation was required varied across the respondents (Madaus, Banerjee, & Hamblet, 2010; see box, "DS and the Professional Connection" on page 74). Schools that really follow the spirit of federal laws governing accommodating the needs of students with disability in the higher education setting will be more likely to accept students' proof of disability without any discussion.

Definition

Psychoeducational testing uses standardized tests and questionnaires to identify a student's strengths and weaknesses in a variety of areas, including but not limited to cognitive development, academic achievement, behavior, and emotion

Do the Requested Accommodations Provide Access to the Curriculum?

The laws in effect at college emphasize providing access to college programs versus success (i.e., high grades). What this means is that colleges may choose to substitute what they deem an equivalent accommodation for one a student has requested. For example, colleges may refuse a student's request for a notetaker, but allow recording lectures with a digital recorder—and may even loan one to the student (see box, "Notes Are Not a Free Pass" on page 75). By doing this, the college provides access to the curriculum through a reasonable accommodation, even if it is not students' accommodation of choice.

Are These Accommodations "Reasonable"?

Colleges do not have to provide accommodations that "fundamentally alter" their programs (28 C.F.R. §35.130[b][7]), so certain kinds of adjustments may simply not be available to students (Madaus, 2009; McGuire, 2009; Shaw, 2009)—especially as regards admissions standards, course requirements, and requirements for majors and graduation. Students typically need to meet two sets of requirements for graduation: the college's general education or distribution requirements, and the requirements for their major. Distribution requirements may include such standards as two semesters each of math, humanities, social science, and science. As explained in Step 1, if colleges can show that they have considered the ramifications of students' requested accommodations and found that these would change their essential academic standards, they can reject them (National Association of College and University Attorneys, 1997). So, if schools believe that 2 years of foreign language is an essential element of their overall degree program, or that Statistics is essential to completing a degree in Psychology, they need not grant waivers or substitutions of such a requirement, even for students with disabilities (see box, "A Word About Waivers and Substitutions" on page 76).

DS and the Professional Connection

Most students are unlikely to encounter any difficulty with being found eligible for services. But sometimes a college will accept a student's documentation of disability and still find that it doesn't show the student needs the requested accommodations (Madaus, 2009). Students with mostly high scores whose lowest scores on psychoeducational testing are far below their other scores might not be eligible for accommodations because they are still functioning in the Average range, even in their area of greatest weakness. It is important for high school professionals to familiarize themselves with eligibility standards at colleges of interest so that they can alert students whose scores might not make them eligible to the possibility that they will not receive services. This way, students can prepare themselves by researching the other sources of support on campus. Students who are not found eligible for services still have access to many support services available on most campuses, such as tutoring, remedial or developmental classes, writing labs, and study skills courses.

The "reasonable" test is also applied to other kinds of requests based on the other three exceptions (i.e., posing an undue burden, concerns about safety, and providing a personal service; see box, "DS and the Parent Connection" on page 77). Students who ask to be tutored by someone who has a degree in a certain subject will find that this request is considered a personal service. Students with autism spectrum disorders or psychological disorders may find that some of their behaviors are (after an individual review of their particular case) considered a threat to safety. This is why it is important for students to make sure that they know, before they go to college, what kinds of accommodations may not be acceptable, especially if these accommodations will require coordinating with an outside agency (e.g., nursing services).

Most colleges would probably agree that their job is to educate students and to grant degrees to those who meet their requirements—but not to guarantee them jobs. Therefore, some schools may be willing to make adjustments to the requirements for their degree programs' practical experiences, even if such adjustments are unlikely to be available when students enter their chosen profession. Other schools may be more resistant to altering the requirements for practical experiences, believing it important to make the internship experience truly reflect the requirements of the employment field. Students who are granted exceptions or adjustments in internship and field work assignments should be aware that these may not be available to them when they seek jobs in their chosen field (see box, "A Word About Choice of Major" on pages 78-79).

How Do Students Request Accommodations?

After they're admitted to college, students typically submit a request for accommodations as part of a larger disability disclosure process. They may either have to attend a meeting with a DS coordinator prepared to ask for accommodations or may have to list their requests for accommodation on a form provided by DS. Any college's

Notes Are Not a Free Pass

The accommodation of getting a copy of classmates' notes is meant to help students with disabilities catch information they may have missed while taking their own notes, not to provide them with an excuse to skip class or do something else while they're in class. Students should be aware that having a notetaker does not mean that they do not have to take their own notes or be attentive in (or show up for) class. First, notetakers' notes may seem really out of context if students have not attended the class and been a part of the discussions. Second, some colleges may require students to show their own notes from a class (to prove that they were present and taking notes) before receiving the ones from the notetaker. In other words, students are still expected to attend classes and get information down as best they can; having a notetaker is not a license to read the campus paper or surf the Internet while sitting through lectures. Receiving copies of a classmates' notes is definitely not a pass out of class: Professors may take attendance, and class participation may count as part of students' grade.

procedure will likely ask students to submit their requests in writing (this helps with clarity and provides a record of the requests, in case students later complain that they didn't receive accommodations for which they asked).

Start Early

Students should initiate the accommodation request process as early as possible— even as soon as they enroll (i.e., as soon as they send in their deposit). From the end of August through the middle of the fall, DS offices are typically inundated with accommodation requests from incoming freshmen. Submitting the documentation (see Step 7) and requests early may permit review of the paperwork over the summer, when DS staff members tend to be less busy and may be able to give it more attention. Applying well before school begins also allows time to provide any additional required information or documentation DS may request, and it increases the likelihood of accommodations being in place when the semester starts.

Be Specific in Making Requests

It is not generally acceptable for students to simply say, "See p. 10 of my testing report. I want all the accommodations listed on that page." Accommodations received in high school may not be relevant or available at the college level. Testing reports also often include recommendations for things students should do for themselves, such as developing study strategies. A student who simply points DS to a page in their report risks coming off as unaware and uninvolved in the process. Although colleges may offer some accommodations that students have not requested, students first have to

A Word About Waivers and Substitutions

When students with disabilities ask an academic department for substitutions or waivers of program or graduation requirements, DS might or might not be consulted about whether such adjustments are appropriate given the students' level of functioning. Even if DS staff is approached, the ultimate decision is in the hands of the academic department and/or the relevant administrators, as the decisions will revolve around the school's or department's essential requirements.

Students concerned about their ability to pass certain classes should make substitution or waiver requests fairly early in their education because, in extreme cases, they might have to transfer to another school if their current college won't waive a class they can't pass. Colleges do not have to waive or offer a substitution for a class just because a student has completed all other requirements and is ready to graduate. Schools may actually make students attempt a difficult class before they will even consider a change to requirements. In some cases, students may need to choose another major, which will likely entail taking and paying for more courses (and possibly not graduating with their class). **This is why it is as important for students to know how they get out of a college as it is for them to know how they get in** (Madaus, 2009, p. 56).

ask for specific adjustments. Note that when submitting an accommodations request, it is perfectly acceptable for students to ask whether they are eligible for any other accommodations of which they might not be aware.

DS and the Parent Connection

A student's parents arrived on campus for the campus tour, and came by our office with questions about disability services that might be available for their daughter. Their daughter had moderately well-managed diabetes, but she occasionally needed emergency insulin injections when her blood sugar became too low; the parents expected faculty and staff to administer these injections as needed. They also stated that she needed soda left in her fridge in the dorm room and a roommate who would check on her at night. If her blood sugar was too low, the parents expected her roommate to assist her in getting a sugar boost, as the low-sugar condition might render her unable to get out of bed. The student's parents requested that the university arrange these services as accommodation for the student's diabetes.

Although I empathized with the parents' concern for their daughter, I could not imagine asking faculty and staff members to administer these injections; this was clearly an unreasonable request. I noted that the student was absent during the request process. Though I explained to the parents that they were requesting personal services that the university was not required to provide, they emphatically insisted that the university had to provide the requested accommodations.

After discussing the differences between high school and college and explaining that college accommodations work differently than they do in the high school special education environment, I provided the parents with a transition letter from the Office for Civil Rights discussing the differences between high school and college. I again suggested that the services they requested were of a personal nature, and not something the university was required to provide. They reported that they had already contacted OCR about their daughter's experience in high school, and they noted how quickly services were changed following the complaint. I finished the conversation by saying that we would attempt to assist their daughter if she came to our school, and hoped that she would be able to manage herself independently while on campus and, if needed, with a personal care assistant—at her expense. I finished the conversation by explaining to the student's parents that she could file an internal grievance about an accommodation issue or file an external complaint with OCR if she was unhappy with my accommodation decision.

I never did hear from the student. For all I know, she may have attended the university without contacting my office. Maybe her parents finally came to understand the limits of reasonable accommodation.

Mikael Snitker,
Assistant Professor and Rehabilitation Counselor,
Ferris State University, Michigan

Before students graduate from high school, they should work with their case manager and parents to compose a list of accommodations to request when they get to college. IEP team members should explain to students how their psychoeducational testing supports their requests, as students may be asked to justify their need for these accommodations. They should know what their diagnosis is, and what their specific symptoms are. They should be able to articulate how each requested accommodation relates to a particular manifestation of their disability (e.g., I need a blank piece of paper to help me keep track on Scantron exams because of my visual tracking problem), though these explanations can be simple and need not be technical. It is a good idea for students to rehearse a discussion of their requested accommodations with their case manager or special education teacher before they graduate.

As part of preparing to request accommodations, students should be able to answer the following questions:

1. What is your disability?

2. What accommodations do you want to request?

A Word About Choice of Major

Colleges can deny students with disabilities entrance to certain programs of study if these students cannot meet the technical requirements for admission to these programs based on the skills, coursework, or class sequence considered important for getting a license or job in the field (Madaus, 2009). An example of this would be requiring Engineering majors to have completed certain math and science courses in order to be accepted to the program. But even when there are no barriers to choosing a program of study, colleges do not have to make any modifications to their curriculum in order to ensure that students who choose a major complete a degree in their chosen field of study. Because they are viewed as adults, students at college have to take the responsibility for making an educated decision about what field of study they should pursue. Students who cannot pass the required classes for a major are not considered qualified for that major and cannot earn a degree in that major at that college (requirements may or may not be different in the same program at another school, which is why research is so important; see Step 6). Students who want to pursue a major whose requirements present a significant challenge should apply for a waiver or substitution early in their academic career. This way, if their request is denied, they can choose a different major, and they won't lose too much time (and money) pursuing a degree whose requirements they can't complete.

Though colleges can bar students from entering degree programs where they don't meet the technical requirements for entrance, and given the fact that colleges don't have to make certain adjustments or allow waivers or substitutions, students and their parents might find it surprising that colleges also can neither advise students not to choose a particular major on the basis of their disability nor prevent them from choosing a particular one (unless they do this for all students). To do so would be discriminatory. Therefore, all students can choose any major for which they meet the admissions requirements—but it is their responsibility to consider whether they can meet all the requirements for that degree.

3. How do these accommodations help you with your specific disability?

4. Have you used these accommodations before?

5. If you have not used them before, why do think you will need them in college?

What Happens Next?

This will vary, depending upon a particular school's process. At some schools, students may have to meet with a DS coordinator after they turn in their paperwork—or they may have to bring their paperwork with them to such a meeting rather than submitting it ahead of time. These meetings are meant to benefit students, as they allow them to interact with DS staff, something that the Department of Education's Office of Civil Rights likes to see (but does not mandate) in schools' accommodation process. These meetings are a chance for students to advocate for themselves and their requests (see Step 3) and to ask questions about what accommodations DS thinks might be appropriate for them that they might not know about.

Students have to take responsibility for researching the requirements for their desired field of study and for deciding whether or not they can pass them. Though academic advisors assigned to them freshman year may be able to help with the research, they are unlikely to know anything about disabilities (and are unlikely to know which students have them, as colleges, to protect students' privacy, probably won't tell advisors which students have disabilities). So they will be unlikely to be able to help students in deciding whether their major is appropriate given their profile of strengths and weaknesses. Once they gather information about a major's requirements, students can ask DS to help them research whether waivers or substitutions have been made in the past, though students should understand that this does not mean that they will receive one.

To some families, it may seem strange that, except in the case of majors with admissions requirements, colleges will not prevent students from choosing a field of study where they risk not being able to complete the requirements. But it's important to remember that colleges don't prevent students without disabilities from pursuing particular majors, and some of these students also will not be able to complete their desired program. Such administrative intervention might be appropriate at the elementary or secondary level, but it isn't at the postsecondary level.

On the bright side, sometimes the numbers (i.e., students' scores on psychoeducational testing) don't tell the whole story. With perseverance and the right kind of tutorial assistance, some students may be able to complete programs of study which are very challenging for them. Colleges would not want to be responsible for keeping a student out of a major they can complete based on assumptions about their abilities (or disabilities).

At some schools, students' requests and their supporting paperwork will then be reviewed by one person who is in charge of this process; at others it may be reviewed by a committee. Federal law does not dictate how this should be done, but there is an expectation that the process will be applied consistently (i.e., that all students with similar impairments will be reviewed by the same person or panel). Applications from students with different disabilities may be reviewed by different people (e.g., there may be a committee to review documentation from students with psychological disabilities, but paperwork from students with medical disabilities might be reviewed by a doctor from Health Services). If students are curious about the process, they should be comfortable asking questions, and DS should answer them (though they may decline to name review committee members, in order to prevent students from trying to lobby these professionals individually).

The format of response may vary, too. Some schools may send students an e-mail telling them the accommodations for which they have been approved, although others may tell them to come pick up their letters of accommodation (see Step 2). When first submitting their accommodation requests, students should ask how they will hear back. This way, they'll know what to expect. They also need to respond to whatever the message from DS tells them to do. Students who ignore an e-mail from DS in their in-box or a letter in their campus mail and later say that they didn't ever hear back about their accommodations and didn't receive the accommodations will have no defense when DS shows them a copy of the message that was sent to them (which DS will keep for its own records).

How Long Does the Process Take?

The law is not specific about how long colleges have to respond to students' requests, so it's hard to say. It really depends upon how many people are involved in the process (some DS offices are one-person operations) and how many students have submitted documentation at that particular time. When they submit their paperwork (or meet with DS staff), students should ask how long the process will take—this is a very appropriate question and will demonstrate their interest in the process. If students don't hear back in a week or two (or in whatever time period they were told it would take), they should definitely follow up with DS to make sure that their paperwork is being reviewed (i.e., confirm that it hasn't been misplaced), and they should feel comfortable asking when they can expect an answer.

How Many Times Do Students Have to Do This?

Once students are approved for accommodations, they do not have to go through the self-identification and documentation process again unless they transfer to another college (which will have its own process) or subsequently request additional accommodations (in which case they may have to provide more documentation, if justification is not seen in what they originally submitted). Students with certain kinds of disabilities (e.g., psychological, medical, ADD) may be required to provide updated information about their condition every year or so. But even in these cases, this usually means submitting a form from a doctor or relevant professional; it does not usually involve the same level of paperwork or time.

What If Students Don't Get the Accommodations They Request?

Though it does not happen very often, students are sometimes found ineligible for services; more commonly, they are found eligible for services but do not receive all of the accommodations they requested. These students can file a grievance if they wish (see Step 2). But before they do something so formal, it's worthwhile to ask the DS office for an additional review (a chance to practice self-advocacy skills in a conflict resolution situation).

Ask for Feedback

Having a meeting will allow students to submit and discuss any additional information and provide the DS representative with examples of how they cope with their disability and why the accommodations they requested are necessary to level the playing field for them. The meeting may allow the DS representative to ask some questions, look at something differently on a second review, or notice a detail that was missed the first time, and decide to approve accommodations. If the requested accommodation falls under any of the four exceptions discussed in Step 1, however, students are likely to have a tough time making a case for these adjustments. But they may certainly try, no matter what reason is given. If students need to provide additional information in order to support their request, they should make sure that they understand exactly what's needed, get this information, and submit it. Depending upon DS's response, students may have to pursue additional testing or get a letter from their doctor providing justification for their request.

Try Alternative Accommodations

In some cases, DS may grant a different accommodation than the one that students requested (e.g., instead of having someone read their exams to them, students may be given permission to have their exams scanned into a computer loaded with text-to-speech software). Colleges see this as providing the access that the law demands, even if it isn't students' preferred accommodation. Students should ask for help and time to practice with technology before their exams, which DS should be happy to give them. But remember that the law does not require schools to grant students' preferred accommodations if they offer a parallel one that offers the same access.

Students who have been granted accommodations different from those they requested should give them a proper try before appealing DS's decision. They may find that the adjustments are just as effective as the ones they initially requested (or perhaps even more effective). They should accept any training or help DS offers to go along with their accommodations. For instance, colleges who loan digital recorders to students instead of granting them notetakers may show them how to use this accommodation effectively (e.g., use the counter rather than listen to entire lectures several times over). Students who choose not to accept this training and later request notetakers again are likely to be asked about how they used the recorder. If their response is "I didn't try," their request is unlikely to receive further review until they actually utilize the approved accommodation (see box, "Dealing With Rejection").

What If Students Need More or Different Accommodations?

Some classes will stress students' learning weaknesses more than others or may introduce barriers not previously anticipated (e.g., a student with a visual impairment who changes majors from Economics to Biology will now have to request a special microscope, something she would not previously have requested). Students can ask for additional accommodations at any time during their education. Depending upon the request, the paperwork they submitted when they first applied for accommodations may be sufficient to document a need for new ones. If not, they will have to supply whatever DS requests, but they will not have to undergo the full process again.

Students who are struggling academically or who are doing well but would like to do better may think that the answer to their distress is to request more accommodations. Again, this can be appropriate in certain circumstances, as in the case of the political science major who switches to physics and now needs to request permission to use a calculator on exams. But students hoping that more academic adjustments

Dealing With Rejection

The path to services and accommodations can be imagined as having two gates. The first one students have to pass through requires the establishment of the presence of a disability. This is the purpose of the documentation (see Step 7), and it is generally considered to be the easier part of the process. The ADA Amendments Act of 2008 was intended to help make this piece much less onerous for students than it may have been in the past (Simon & Lissner, 2011). The next gate students have to get through involves demonstrating that their disability creates a substantial limitation in their functioning. This is where some students might encounter some difficulty.

If they are not found eligible at all, or denied an accommodation they feel they really need, it behooves students to first try the least-confrontational route of asking DS again for accommodation and providing any additional information requested. Setting up a meeting to discuss the request could be a good idea, as DS staff may ask them something in the conversation that will allow them to respond in a way that makes their case, or they just may explain themselves better in a conversation than in a written request. This is a very adult way of dealing with a problem, and it's good practice for their future in the work world. However, as Step 2 mentioned, students can also file a grievance—although they need to be aware that grievance processes are likely to take more time than the regular DS review process. And students should keep in mind that, when it comes to granting and denying accommodations, the law grants colleges a lot of discretion (McGuire, 2009).

will boost their performance need to keep two things in mind. One is that research does not support the notion that getting more accommodations equals improved academic performance (Trammell, 2003). The other is that colleges are not required to provide enough accommodations to either allow them to perform like their peers or to allow for mastery of the materials (Legal Roundup, 2009a). A better choice for these students is likely to be seeking help at the tutoring center on campus (see box, "What Help Does a College Tutoring Center Provide?" on page 84).

What Accommodations Should Students Request?

Knowing that accommodations may be different at college, how do students know what to request? As with everything else, the appropriateness is judged on an individual basis. Table 5-1 on pages 91-94 provides a list of commonly requested accommodations, with some information regarding how they are may be viewed or evaluated.

Sometimes students' requests demonstrate a lack of knowledge about the college environment and what accommodations are appropriate there.

This is not the image most students would want to project, so they should understand what requests they should avoid, and why:

- *Small class sizes.* This is not a postsecondary disability accommodation; it is something students should look for in a college as they conduct their search.

- *Extra time with professors.* This is what office hours are for (see Step 4). Students may have to sign up for a slot or wait on line like everyone else; DS will not arrange a special time for them to meet with professors.

- *Quiet study space.* Students can find this at the library, and some dorms may have quiet study rooms. This is not something DS will arrange.

- *Preferential seating.* Seats are not usually assigned at college. If students want to sit in the front close to where the professor lectures, they need to get to class a bit early (they are unlikely to find much competition for the front row).

- *Advanced notice of assignments.* Course syllabi generally indicate deadlines for assignments as well as exam dates. Students who want more specific information about assignments should ask their professors directly.

- *Information about exam format.* This is not an accommodation. Students who want to know in advance whether they will be taking an essay or multiple-choice exam should ask their professors, though it is likely that professors will give the whole class this information anyway a week or so ahead of time.

- *Progress reports.* This is not a responsibility of anyone at the college, though some colleges may provide them. If students want to periodically know how they are doing, they should ask professors directly. They should also create a system for tracking their grades so that they don't need to ask anyone how they are doing; they will have all of the information they need right at their fingertips.

- *Waiver of final exam.* Most schools would view this as a fundamental alteration of a course.

Submitting a lengthy list of accommodations is not necessarily to a student's advantage; there is no law that says that colleges have to grant a certain portion or percentage of students' requests. Certainly, it would make sense for the number of accommodations that students request to be somewhat proportionate to their degree of impairment (see box, "A Word About Accommodations" on page 85). When composing their list of accommodations to request, students should remember that colleges expect students to demonstrate not just a certain level of self-sufficiency but also a degree of self-knowledge. Students' accommodation requests must be directly related to their areas of weakness, and the students must understand them and agree that they will be helpful (which means that they should discuss these requests with their IEP team before they graduate from high school).

Professionals who do evaluations should also keep this point in mind when they write testing reports for students transitioning to college. And they should make a distinction between the recommendations for accommodations that colleges grant and arrange and strategies that they think students should utilize independently to improve academic performance. This will make the request process (see Figure 5-1 on page 95) easier for students when they get to college, and reinforce for them the idea that their success depends largely upon the effort they are willing to expend.

What Help Does a College Tutoring Center Provide?

Students can typically expect a tutor at the campus academic support center to help them plan their assignments and organize their notes, and also check their drafts for logic and flow. However, at some schools, they will not go much farther than this. Students should expect to use spell- and grammar-check tools on their own; all students, regardless of disability, are expected to check their papers over before handing them in. The amount of help students receive in creating and editing their drafts may vary from tutor to tutor or change based on the philosophy of the tutoring center. The bottom line is that at most colleges, the most basic forms of help for assignments is the same for all students regardless of whether they have a disability, and such help is not considered an accommodation. It is simply up to students to make appointments for as much tutoring as they think they need—and the responsibility is theirs alone.

What About Assistive Technology and Technology Accommodations?

Table 5-2 on page 96 describes several products often used to help individuals with disabilities bypass their areas of difficulty (Banerjee, 2009). Although a few are special technologies designed to bypass specific disabilities, the rest are marketed to and used by the general public—a point that should be stressed to students who resist, thinking that these technologies mark them as having disabilities. These tools can be a huge help with reading loads and assignments and may allow students to work much more quickly in college. Becoming fluent with these technologies while they are still in high school means that students don't need to spend time learning how to use them once they're at college and faced with course assignments.

Colleges cannot charge approved students for accommodations such as the conversion of their textbooks to an alternative format. They also can't charge them to use the technology (such as software) that they have in their office or the library. However, students should know that colleges do not have to offer students a copy of such software (or their own personal scanner) to use in their dorm rooms; they will have to use such items within the limits of the DS office's or library's hours. Students who want to use these technologies on their own time in their own room will have to purchase the software or equipment. Similarly, colleges may offer to students, at no charge, access to books in alternative formats through their institutional membership to libraries or organizations that provide these. However, if the format provided isn't designed for use with computers, students will have to purchase or lease their own special players in order to make use of these technologies back in their dorm room.

What If Students Don't Want to Request Accommodations?

Every year, a certain number of students with disabilities go to college and decide not to self-identify (see box, "Can I Outgrow My Disability?" on pages 86-87). This is students' right, but it is also their "right" to live with any consequences that result from them deciding not to request accommodations (Madaus, 2009). Before students head to college, they should have a serious discussion with their families and any relevant professionals about this decision.

A Word About Accommodations

Accommodations are not a "magic bullet." In other words, the effectiveness of accommodations depends upon how relevant the accommodations are to the student's learning problems (Trammell, 2003). This is why it is so important that students try different accommodations in high school, in order to make sure that these actually work for them. Accommodations are also not a substitute for hard work. For instance, having more time to sit for an exam for which they have not prepared will not boost their grade. This is why development of academic skills and study and compensatory strategies should be a high priority in students' high school plans.

Not receiving needed accommodations can result in students' making a poor performance on midterms and finals—or even doing well, but not as well as they could have. And students who don't maintain the minimum grade point average (GPA) required by the college may be put on academic probation (McGuire, 2009). Those who don't bring their grades up during this probationary period should expect to be dismissed from the college if that's the college's policy. Some students, after experiencing these types of problems, will decide to request accommodations. The down side of this is that generally colleges will not allow students to retake exams and the poor initial grades will remain on the student's record. Colleges do not need to readmit students who have been dismissed, even if students reveal a previously undisclosed disability (Legal Roundup, 2008a). And those schools that do give students another chance do not have to readmit them with a blank slate (McGuire, 2009).

As long as they are willing to live with any consequences that result from this choice, students can choose to delay their request for accommodations as long as they like (Madaus, 2009). Some students like to "try" their first set of exams without accommodations, then decide that they want to apply for them afterward. They should know that colleges cannot put a limit on when students can apply for accommodations; it can happen anytime during their education, even the second semester of their senior year. However, colleges can tell students that it will take them some time to review their

Can I Outgrow My Disability?

In a National Longitudinal Transition Study-2 report, more than half of the students who had completed high school and enrolled in some form of postsecondary education and who had been diagnosed with a disability did not consider themselves to have a disability (Newman, Wagner, Cameto, & Knokey, 2009). How is this possible? How is it that students who have received special education services their whole lives do not have disabilities when they go to college?

In some districts, students are placed in special education and receive accommodations in the early grades because they are developmentally behind their classmates. By the time they leave high school, some of these students have caught up in their former areas of weakness and perform on a level comparable to their peers, although they may continue to retain their special education status. The recent response-to-intervention approach that has been promulgated over the past few years is partially intended to identify these "late bloomers" and provide them with increasing levels of support and different kinds of remediation activities without placing them in the special education system (Fuchs & Fuchs, 2006), in order to avoid misdiagnosing students as having learning disabilities. However, not all districts take this approach.

Once students are identified as requiring special education services and an IEP is developed, some districts may continue to provide the same accommodations and services every year without questioning the need for them or place students on Section 504 plans for monitoring purposes (Madaus, 2005). Districts are no longer required to retest students every few years as they used to, as long as the school and parents agree that no additional testing is necessary to determine their needs (Madaus & Shaw; 2007 McGuire, 2009). As documentation and requests, so those who decide to wait until the day before finals start are likely to end up taking their tests without accommodations (Madaus, 2009). But students should know that if they don't apply for accommodations when they enter as freshmen, this does not preclude them from asking for them at a later time.

What Accommodations Do Students Really Need?

Choosing Accommodations: Self-Assessment and Self-Knowledge Are Key

As part of the college search process (see Step 6), students should consider how much support they will need in college. Within the structured setting of high school, some students may not have needed certain accommodations (e.g., notetaking), so they may be hesitant to ask for these in college. But if students and their advisors (i.e., high school professionals and parents) think that certain accommodations they have not yet used may be helpful for the first time in college, students should request these, as long as they are able to defend their requests by explaining how the accommodation would help them access the curriculum or material. An ability to discuss this articulately will also demonstrate to DS that students understand that the environment they are entering is different from the one to which they are accustomed.

a result, however, there is no regular tracking of students' strengths and challenges and whether they do, in fact, have learning disabilities. These students, having caught up to their peers academically by the time they graduate, may not have psychoeducational testing scores that qualify them for accommodations when they get to college. For their part, these students may not even ask for accommodations, as they may know intuitively that they don't need support, or they may not have been using the accommodations written into their IEP.

In other instances, students who are struggling in school but do not qualify for an IEP may receive support through a 504 plan during their elementary and secondary education as a "consolation prize" (Madaus, 2009, p. 42). There are many good things about districts' wanting to help students who need support even if they do not meet the requirements for special education. However, receiving this type of (often minimal) support may raise an unrealistic expectation that these students will be eligible for similar services at college. These students, too, may realize that they were given a 504 plan as an exception, and may not feel the need to ask for accommodations at college (or may be reluctant to because they know they don't have a strong case).

High school staff and parents sometimes assume that positive student progress is the result of the accommodations and help from special education teachers. Indeed, this may be the case. On the other hand, students may be doing better because they have learned strategies and techniques that mitigate the effect of their disability. The "scaffolding" provided by the IEP or Section 504 plan may no longer be necessary. But if no one asks students what is helping them to succeed—is it accommodations or their own strategies?— they may not realize that they no longer require certain accommodations or, perhaps, any support at all.

Conversely, students might choose to do without other accommodations they have been using, or request accommodations only in certain classes (Madaus, 2009). For instance, a student with a math disability may not require any accommodations in an American History class. This type of self-assessment—"What support do I need, and in what type of setting?"—adds to self-knowledge and, by making this a subjective process, can also can motivate students who may otherwise be reluctant to seek accommodation (i.e., they are trying to shed the "disability" portion of their identity, not an uncommon phenomenon for students transitioning to college). Students will be best able to make a good judgment in these instances if they've had the opportunity to develop self-knowledge throughout high school (see Step 2). Asking students for their feedback on the usefulness of their accommodations will help professionals and parents to find out what accommodations students do and do not find helpful, and offer a chance to consider other accommodations that might be of use (Madaus, 2009). It will also allow adults a chance to offer students feedback about their view of students' skills and ability to cope without certain accommodations.

Developing Self-Reliance Through Eliminating Accommodations

Throughout their high school years, college-bound students' long-term goals should include developing and utilizing effective study techniques and strategies (see Step 4) that help them to bypass their learning difficulties—and students' accommodations and instruction should reflect this goal (Madaus, 2009; Shaw, 2009). Students should be working toward independence; the shift should be from teachers doing things for students to students taking ownership of their learning and materials. Understanding the kinds of accommodations available at college can help to inform this process, and students will be better prepared for the postsecondary environment if the accommodations they use are similar to those available at college (McGuire, 2009; Shaw, 2009). For example, rather than relying on a paraprofessional to touch a student on the shoulder and redirect him, the student might learn to use a watch that vibrates quietly on his wrist to bring his attention back to class every few minutes (see box, "Real Life: Letting Go of Accommodations" on page 89). Students who truly cannot concentrate without a human aide to refocus them every few minutes might want to consider alternatives to a traditional 4-year college environment, as this type of classroom assistance is not generally considered appropriate in this kind of setting. Even if this accommodation is allowed, students have to hire their own assistants to perform this function, and if their attention problems or the actions of the assistant disrupt the class, the college may argue that the accommodation is not reasonable. Products, such as the Watchminder 3, offer stopwatch, countdown functions, vibration, and audible alerts.

      http://watchminder.com/

Parents and students may balk at pulling some accommodations that result in lower grades. But are these accommodations helping the student to prepare for college (Banerjee & Brinckerhoff, 2009)? It does not matter whether good grades get a student into college if she does not have the work habits and skills to stay enrolled there. Considering alternative accommodations that emphasize independence may not result in the highest GPA, but it will give students a more realistic sense of their abilities and help them to develop the important independent study and self-assessment skills they will need in college.

Accommodations that students can utilize by themselves and that are likely to be available at college should be the focus of high school planning. Caution should be used in choosing accommodations that will not be available at college (such as a reduction in page length for essays), as allowing students to utilize these adjustments will not help them to prepare for the college environment (Madaus, 2009; Shaw, 2009). If there are serious concerns about students' making progress without some very supportive accommodations, IEP teams can consider the option of starting students with such accommodations early in students' high school years with the stated goal of eliminating them by junior year. If students' academic performance seriously suffers (not just a drop from a B to a C, but a B to an F), then accommodations should be reinstated, but the team should also talk about additional postsecondary alternatives to the traditional 4-year school. Students who are seriously considering entering the traditional college environment need to become accustomed to the adjustments that colleges may offer, and should see if they can perform without those that will not be available (Shaw, 2009).

There is one more good reason for students to pare down their accommodation requests to only what they truly need to have a level playing field in the college environment. College can be considered a "dress rehearsal" for life. It is the last place where students have access to accommodations with relative ease. After college, students who need accommodations in the work place will have to self-advocate (see Step 2) with their employers. Obviously, once they are out of the academic environment, many will not need many adjustments, as they will likely select jobs that stress their areas of strength. But it is a good idea to learn the difference between which accommodations are necessary to complete tasks, and which are helpful but not essential.

Real Life: Letting Go of Accommodations

Debra Bromfield, a public-school special education director, offers a story from her work in a different district to illustrate the importance of developing students' skills through the careful use of accommodations. "Tom" started his education in self-contained classes; he was gradually placed in inclusion classes. He learned to take notes, first through the use of templates, and then on his own. Though he started school with a one-on-one aide, this accommodation was phased out as Tom was gradually moved to classes where there was already support in place. By senior year, he was independently accessing his education and attending an academic support class daily. Adults facilitated his participation in group activities, but this too was eventually phased out. In the end, Tom transitioned to community college and made the dean's list. When he returned to his old high school to speak about his college experiences at a school event, Tom's mother approached Bromfield to say that she had never believed he could be so successful.

Summary

One of the best reasons to put so much consideration into students' accommodations early in their high school years is that the results of any experimentation and/or discussions will help to inform students' college search. As Step 6 will discuss, services and accommodations can vary widely from school to school. Early in their high school years, students need to get a realistic sense of how much support they will need in college so that they can make sure that the schools to which they apply will provide the services they will need to be successful.

Table 5-1. Commonly Requested Accommodations (1 of 4)

Request	Comments
Reduced course load	• Can be a very appropriate accommodation, especially in students' first semester; it can help in the overall adjustment to the academic demands and new living environment. • Might be offered as a "more appropriate" accommodation to students who request extended deadlines for assignments. • If students with disabilities can't maintain their student insurance plan on a part-time schedule, Michelle's Law (2008) allows them to stay on their family's health insurance policy (a big concern for most families). • Students concerned about graduating on time can take classes during winter or summer breaks to maintain progress.
Notetaking	• Colleges may be particular about who gets this if they believe that the ability to decide what information in a lecture is the most salient and get it down on paper or in electronic form is a lifelong skill that students need to acquire. • Might only be offered to students with a significant disability or more than one disability that interferes with notetaking. • Many notetakers are student volunteers, not professionals or teachers, so note quality may vary. • Possible substitutions: digitally recording classes/lectures, notetaking workshops for students with disabilities. • If colleges are providing transcription for a student with a hearing impairment in the same class, they might also provide the transcript to other students with disabilities.
Private dorm room	• Burden of proof that a single room is necessary to provide access is often a heavy one; many colleges hold that sharing a room during freshman year is an integral part of the college educational experience. • A number of schools consistently experience housing shortages, which can affect the availability of single rooms. • Students with serious physical disabilities might be accommodated with a double room for which they are not charged the single room premium if they need noisy, bulky medical equipment or frequent visits from an aide. • Students who ask for a single room so they can study in peace will likely instead be directed to the library or dorm quiet room. • Colleges might refuse single rooms for students with social difficulties because they want to prevent them from being at risk for further isolation.
Priority registration	• Appropriate for students with medications that have peak effectiveness at certain points during the day or whose meds may interfere with sleep if they take them late in the day in order to focus in night classes. • Also appropriate for students who need some time between classes because their disability or medications cause fatigue.
Copies of professors' notes	• DS cannot demand that professors turn over copies of their notes, which are considered intellectual property. • Some professors post their notes on the Internet. When they do, students are welcome to download them, but DS will not do it for them (though DS will show them how to do this the first time if they do not know how).

Table 5-1. Commonly Requested Accommodations (2 of 4)

Request	Comments
Flexibility in attendance	• Can be appropriate for students who experience severe, acute episodes as a result of their psychological or medical disability. • If approved, students may have to follow some sort of protocol as a way of letting DS—and, by extension, their professors—know that they are experiencing a severe episode and are unable to attend classes. • Attendance policy is generally dictated by the professor and/or the department; even when students have very legitimate reasons for missing classes, the requirements for class attendance may be flexible only to a point. • Students unable to attend the required number of classes may have to withdraw or take an incomplete grade and retake the course in a subsequent semester.
Study guides	• Not likely to be approved. • Students are expected to know how to go through their notes and readings, think about what their professors discussed in class, and figure out what they should study. • Although tutoring center staff might help students organize their notes, they are not responsible for putting together study guides. • Students may find it helpful to organize or join a study group to find out what other students think is likely to be on the exam, and they may get some information about topics to be covered on their exams by attending professors' office hours and asking questions.
Extended deadlines on assignments, projects, or papers	• Unlikely to be approved. • Reduced course load may be offered as an alternative accommodation (students should consider asking for this instead of extensions). • Colleges will offer extensions to any student in a crisis (e.g., death of a parent), but many will refuse this as a blanket accommodation for disability. • Students with difficulty meeting deadlines should utilize technology, tutoring, and other relevant services to keep on top of deadlines. • Reason often cited for refusing this accommodation is that students then end up behind in their classes, and when new papers are assigned before the old ones are done students get overwhelmed and anxious. • DS may suggest that students seek help from the campus tutoring center to learn to manage time and deadlines.
Alternative assignments, reduced assignment length, reduced reading load	• Unlikely to be approved. • Likely to be viewed as fundamentally altering college programs. • Students with difficulty completing assignments should utilize technology, tutoring and other relevant services to keep themselves performing at the level expected of them at college.

Table 5-1. Commonly Requested Accommodations (3 of 4)

Request	Comments
Assistance with assignments	• Help with editing, proofreading, and organizing is considered a personal service, which colleges don't have to offer. • Such help is typically offered through college tutoring centers—open to all students—but colleges don't have to go beyond this for students with disabilities. • Some schools may provide this sort of support outside of the usual tutorial supports—for a fee.
Alternative testing methods	• Requests for multiple choice test instead of an essay or an essay instead of multiple choice test, open-book tests, word banks, oral instead of paper exams, and completing a project instead of an exam are likely to be viewed as fundamental alterations (*Wynne v. Tufts University,* 1991, 1992). • Colleges may reject because of concerns over fairness (e.g., student granted an essay exam instead of a multiple-choice exam later complains that his exam was harder than the one his classmates took).
Extended time on exams	• Time and a half for exams is a commonly approved accommodation (although there's no science behind this timeframe). • Students should be specific in how much time they are requesting. (i.e., time and a half or double time); they should keep in mind what their requests will mean: for example, a 3-hour exam now becomes a 6-hour exam. Do they need/want this much time? • Students should not request "untimed" exams, as this is not reasonable (e.g., a student could demand a week for each exam). • If students need short breaks during testing instead of extended time actually working on exams, they should specify this in their request. • Students approved for this may have to take their exams in a separate location from their class, which means access to professors to ask questions may be sacrificed; they should ask about this on a case-by-case basis if they are concerned.
Reader for exams	• Many colleges are moving toward using technology rather than human readers to accommodate students with print-related disabilities; students may be accommodated by taking exams on a computer that reads tests aloud to them. Using technology for exams promotes students' independence, cuts down on DS's personnel costs, and eliminates the worries associated with proctoring (i.e., answering more questions than the professor wants). • Students should ask for training on DS's scanners and text-to-speech software before their exams in order to be ready for their tests. • Students approved for this may have to take their exams in a separate location from their class, which means access to professors to ask questions may be sacrificed; they should ask about this on a case-by-case basis if they are concerned. • Students who want to demonstrate their knowledge of the college environment can ask for "a reader for exams or, if available, use of speech-to-text technology for exams."

Table 5-1. Commonly Requested Accommodations (4 of 4)

Request	Comments
Using a laptop for exams	• It may be difficult to prove that this is necessary to provide access, especially in classes where students take essay exams; colleges may require students to have a significant disability or a number of relevant disabilities. • Even when a laptop has been approved, students will likely have to use one supplied by DS (rather than their own), and it will be disconnected from the Internet. • Students who have specially adapted laptops because of their physical disabilities generally will be allowed to use their own laptops because it eliminates the need for accommodations such as a human scribe. • Students may instead be accommodated with a small keyboard that has a an LCD screen that allows them to view a few words as a time as they type (e.g., Alphasmart). • Students who just need a spelling or grammar checker for exams should ask for this (and extended time to use it) instead of a laptop, as the less complicated request is more likely to be approved. • Students approved for this may have to take their exams in a separate location from their class, which means access to professors to ask questions may be sacrificed; they should ask about this on a case-by-case basis if they are concerned.
Using a calculator for exams	• Not likely to be approved on tests or in classes evaluating calculation skill as it would represent a fundamental alteration. • May be allowed for all students—with or without disabilities—in certain math and science fields because the emphasis is on choosing and utilizing the correct formula, not calculation skill.
Reduced-distraction environment for exams	• A commonly approved accommodation. • Students should avoid asking for a distraction–free testing site, as this is impossible to create. • It is likely that another student may also be in the testing room, as well as a proctor (unless the testing room has cameras to check for cheating). • Students approved for this may have to take their exams in a separate location from their class, which means access to professors to ask questions may be sacrificed; they should ask about this on a case-by-case basis if they are concerned.
Scribes/ speech-to-text technology	• Most likely to be approved for students with physical impairments that limit use of their hands. • Speech-to-text technology may be appropriate substitution for a human scribe (except for students whose voices cannot be understood by such technology, as may happen with students with a severe stutter). • Students should ask for training on DS's speech-to-text software before their exams in order to be ready for their tests. • Proctors or scribes only record students' responses; they do not rephrase or change students' answers in any way. • Students who want to demonstrate their knowledge of the college environment can ask for "a scribe for exams" or, if available, use of text-to-speech technology for exams. • Students approved for this may have to take their exams in a separate location from their class, which means access to professors to ask questions may be sacrificed; they should ask about this on a case-by-case basis if they are concerned.

Figure 5.1 Accommodation Request Review

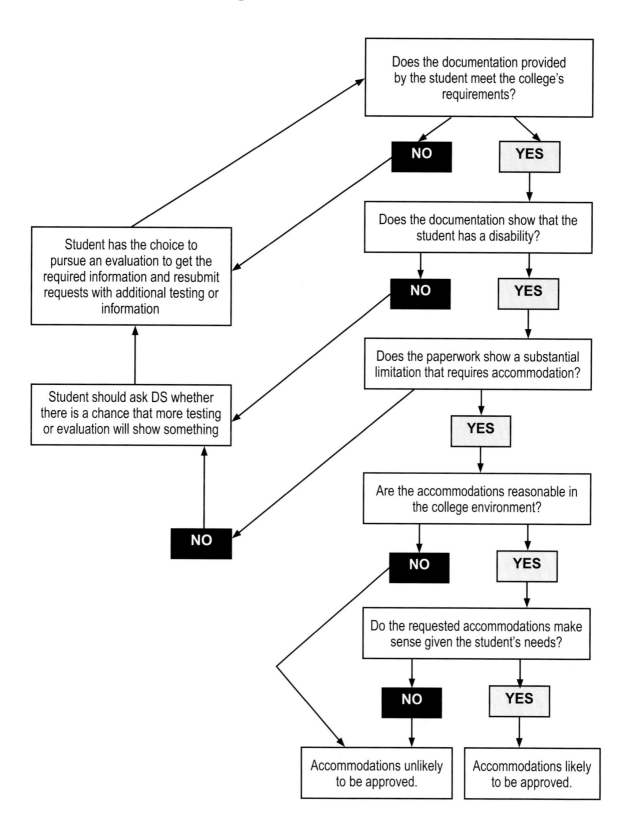

Table 5-2. Assistive Technology Examples

Type of product	Examples/Sources	Comments
Alternative-format books	• Books on CD • DAISY digital talking books • Books in mp3 format (Learning Ally, www.learningally.org, and Bookshare, www.bookshare.org) • Braille • Large print	• Some formats (e.g., DAISY) allow students to listen to books and have computer highlight words as they are read. • Students who feel awkward about having accommodations can use their mp3 players to listen to books that are converted into this format, so no one will know what they are doing.
Text-to-speech programs	• Kurzweil 300 www.kurzweiledu.com/ • Wynn • www.freedomscientific.com/ lsg/ products/wynn.asp • Read & Write GOLD www.texthelp.com/	• Many programs offer features such as dictionaries and the opportunity to highlight and create word lists for further study.
Spelling software	• Ginger www.gingersoftware.com	• Specially designed for students with dyslexia. • Must be connected to Internet, which means it can't be used on exams.
Word prediction software	• Co-Writer www.donjohnston.com/products/ cowriter/index.html • EZ Keys www.words-plus.com/website/ products/soft/ ezkeys.htm	• Some programs offer a variety of spellings for a word based on the first few letters typed, whereas others make predictions based on words already typed; some include text-to-speech features.
Digital recorders and notetaking supports	• Pulse Smartpen www.livescribe.com/en-us/ • MyScript www.visionobjects.com/en/ webstore/ myscript-for-livescribe/description/ • Microsoft OneNote http://office.microsoft.com/en-us/ onenote/	• Students may have to sign an agreement about how they will use such recordings (in order protect professors' intellectual property). • Professors can deny use at times that they also deny notetaking (as when students discuss very personal matters in class).

Step 6

Find the Right College

College-bound students with disabilities need to fully research potential schools, including what sort of supports they offer. College tours and interviews provide a first-hand experience and help determine the "fit" of the school. During the admissions process, students need to decide if and when to disclose their disability. The experience of professionals involved in educating students with disabilities can be helpful in understanding how to compile an application that presents the student in the best light.

Step 6

Find the Right College

It is very exciting when students are accepted to their first-choice school. But some students discover—only after they are enrolled at college—that the school they have chosen to attend does not offer the services and accommodations they need for their success. This kind of disconnect between students' expectations and the actual services available to them should not—and does not—have to happen to anyone. The best way to avoid this kind of situation is for students to incorporate researching disability services as an important part of their college search.

Researching Schools

Make a Target List

There are two basic approaches students can use to develop a target list of colleges. In Method 1, students work with a guidance counselor, college advisor, or transition specialist to compose a list of target schools based on the features most students typically consider (e.g., location, field of study, total enrollment, college culture, social life, activities). For students who have mobility impairments but no learning issues, additional elements like location (i.e., climate) and physical layout will likely be emphasized. Students with moderate disabilities who have used minimal accommodations throughout high school will likely not need extensive services, so their search will likely focus on the usual priorities students focus on during their search. There is a variety of online tools to help with college searches and career/degree choices, including:

Peterson's Education Planner:

                                    www.educationplanner.org/

College Confidential:

                                    www.collegeconfidential.com/

My College Options:

                                    www.mycollegeoptions.org/Home

Princeton Review:

www.princetonreview.com/colleges-majors.aspx

The College Board:

www.collegeboard.org/

ACT:

www.actstudent.org/

Students who utilize numerous accommodations and receive a lot of help and structure from the adults in their lives should probably consider Method 2. This approach begins with creating a list of schools that cater to students with disabilities or provide a variety of service levels, and then winnowing down this list based on the criteria used in Method 1. In addition to using information from their high school counselors or advisors and guides such as Peterson's *Colleges for Students With Learning Disabilities or AD/HD* (2007) and *The K&W Guide to Colleges for Students With Learning Disabilities or ADHD* (Kravets & Wax, 2010), students can identify schools by conducting Internet searches using a combination of the following terms: colleges, students, disabilities, support, structure, programs. Many state departments of education have compiled lists of "disability-friendly" colleges or links to public postsecondary institutions' disability services (DS) offices. The National Center on Secondary Education and Transition continually updates its State Transition Resources page, with links to state transition office resources, at:

www.ncset.org/stateresources/resources.asp

Banerjee & Brinckherhoff (2009) advised against using Method 2 because of concerns that parents will drive the search towards very supportive schools without consideration for how well such colleges will suit the student on other compatibility points (e.g., desired field of study, size, etc.). Just as it would be inadvisable for students to choose a college without giving any thought to the supports available, it is an equally poor idea to choose a college just because it provides a lot of support, which they may not even need, when the rest of the college environment may not be a good match for them (e.g., choosing a supportive school in a rural setting when the student wants to live in a city). Students who utilize Method 2 should bear Banerjee & Brinckerhoff's concerns in mind as they conduct their search.

Investigate Colleges in Depth

After compiling a target list, students can start investigating these colleges more thoroughly. It's important for students (rather than parents) to take the lead in this process as another opportunity to develop and use their self-determination skills. Taking ownership of the college application process encourages and supports student independence.

The process of researching different colleges' services in more depth—in addition to collecting basic information about the setting, size, and course offerings—should answer the following questions (see Table 6-1):

1. Does the college have a dedicated disability services (DS), office or is the responsibility for arranging accommodations part of someone's larger job (e.g., the Dean of Academic Affairs)?

2. Who provides support to students?

3. What kinds of support does the college provide?

4. Are there other resources for academic help?

It can be helpful to record the results of the research on a form specific to each college (see Table 6-2 on pages 121-122). The HEATH Resource Center maintains a portal for resources on college search and planning at:

 www.heath.gwu.edu/resources/links/postsecondary-education-resources

Table 6-1. Investigating Colleges Through Online Research

Question	Comments
Does the college have a Disability Services office?	• From the college's main web page, type *disability services* into the search engine. • If some sort of Disability Services Office or department doesn't appear in search results, try: *academic center, academic success center, academic support, access, diversity, equity, learning center, learning disabilities, learning resource center, learning support, special programs.* • Services may be coordinated through the dean's office or a counseling or learning center, or through the Student Life or Student Services office.
Who provides support to students?	• Take note of contact information for the office (phone number, e-mail address, name of main contact person). • Check to see if the DS page offers information about the background of the staff members: Do any of them have a degree in Special Education or a related field? Have they worked in the disabilities field?
What kinds of support do they provide?	• Record any information the page lists regarding commonly provided accommodations or services. • Do they offer study skills classes or time management seminars? • See whether they mention what types of adaptive technology are available.
Are there other resources for academic help?	• Look for links to other resources for academic help (e.g., math tutoring center, writing center). • Who staffs these help centers? Is it other undergraduate students? Graduate students in specific fields of study?

Understanding the Levels of Service Colleges Provide

Students should know that there are only a few colleges in the whole country that are exempt from providing disability accommodations (U.S. Department of Education, 2007). Students concerned that they are looking at one of these colleges can use the Internet to check for a DS office or call the main switchboard to establish whether there is someone on campus in charge of helping students with disabilities.

Federal law doesn't define what college disability services should look like, who should run them, and what they should include (McGuire, 2009). As mentioned before, colleges may not have an office whose sole purpose is to work with students with disabilities. This may be a function of the tutoring or academic support center, or the responsibility for processing paperwork and approving and arranging accommodations may be assigned to an administrator or tutoring center director as one of many job functions (Elksnin & Elksnin, 2009). Even when there is a full center with lots of staff, it's possible that neither the director nor the staff members have experience or an education in working with students with disabilities (Banerjee & Brunckerhoff, 2009; Elksnin & Elksnin, 2009). This does not mean that these professionals don't do a good job and that they can't be very helpful; it just means that students should understand what the law requires. If it is important to them to attend a college where DS staff is knowledgeable and experienced in disability-related fields, they will have to ask some specific questions during their college research.

In supporting students with disabilities, some colleges provide the minimum level of support required by law—and some go far beyond the minimum, sometimes for free, and sometimes for a fee. It is important for students to decide what level of service they will need at college, and to do their research to make sure that the college they attend has the services they expect.

Level I Services

Schools that provide only what is required by the law offer "compliance-level" services, also referred to as *Level I services* by many guides and web sites. Compliance-level services typically include supports such as text conversion, notetakers, and so forth, and exam accommodations (Banerjee & Brinckerfhoff, 2009; Elsknin & Elksnin, 2009, McGuire, 2009), as well as Brailled texts, sign language interpreting, and so forth, for students with visual or hearing impairments. Level I services usually do not include options like strategy instruction or special advising.

Level II Services

Colleges providing Level II services may offer special classes in study skills and time management or one-on-one time with a learning specialist or academic coach to help students learn study strategies, gain an understanding of their learning profiles, develop self-advocacy skills, and use compensatory techniques—typically for free. Families should know that these "specialists" or "coaches" do not necessarily have graduate degrees in special education or a related field; sometimes these staff members simply receive training from the head of the learning center or DS office—and this person may not be specially trained, either. The law does not require that people serving this function at colleges be certified, experienced, or educated in any way, even if colleges are charging money for their services. Students who wish to check the training of people labeled "specialists" or "coaches" at a college can check the programs' web site, which may provide this information, or call the programs and ask questions of someone who works there. However, a lack of a professional special education background does not mean that these individuals cannot be of help to students with disabilities; in fact, many of these professionals are great at working with students. What it means is that students looking at these special programs need to ask specific questions so that they can be sure that they understand what services are available to students at the college, and who will be providing those services. Because they don't charge extra fees for increased services, schools with Level II services are typically the most difficult to find.

Level III Services

Some colleges offer even more expanded fee-for-service programs in addition to or instead of Level II services (though some Level III services may resemble some of the more supportive Level II programs). These may include content-area tutoring, specialized academic or career advising, or targeted support for specific disabilities. For example, some colleges offer ADD coaching for students on an individual basis. These specialized programs can cost several thousand dollars a semester in addition to baseline college costs, so students who are considering them should make sure that they are educated consumers. They should ask questions about both the content of the program and the training of the individuals who work with students because—as with Level I and Level II services—there are no legal requirements for who fills these positions (regardless of how much the colleges charge students to participate) and there is no guarantee (unless the college offers one) that the staff members have graduate degrees in learning disabilities, training in coaching students with disabilities, or experience working with older (i.e., high school- or college-age) students (see box, "Investigating Level III Services" on page 103).

In addition to asking about who staffs the programs, it is important to ask what services the programs provide, and how frequently students can access such support. The ultimate goal of a program may be to eventually reduce the number of consultations students require during a semester or to wean them off of some kinds of support altogether. Colleges are preparing students for "the real world," so even very supportive programs may be geared toward teaching students self-sufficiency. At some schools, even students who are willing to pay extra may not get a chance to have more sessions per week. If students need more help than the special program provides, they will have to find and pay a commercial entity or individual for these services. This is why it's important to ask questions during students' research.

For many students, Level I services—available everywhere—will be sufficient to meet their needs. Students who work on a daily or weekly basis with a tutor or coach or who have parents who provide them with a lot of structure should consider whether they will require Level II or Level III services in order to make a successful start at college.

Learning About and Understanding Graduation Requirements

When they research colleges, students should give as much consideration to how they will *get out* of a college as they do to how they will *get in*. It is always thrilling for students to get accepted to the college of their choice, but acceptance is meaningless if the student cannot pass the required classes to graduate. As discussed in Step 5, this is why students' college search process must include reviewing graduation requirements:

- Can the student reasonably be expected to meet them?

- If not, does the college have a process for/allow course substitutions?

- Does the college frequently make these substitutions?

Although the DS office might be more able to answer these questions than the Admissions Office (see box, "What Does Admissions Know?" on page 104), students should remember that substitutions or waivers are generally made on a case-by-case basis by the academic department. For example, substitution of a Logic class for the required Calculus class would be evaluated by the Mathematics Department. Students should not go to college expecting to receive a waiver (Madaus, 2003) unless they

---

Investigating Level III Services

Students interested in Level III support services need to do additional, more focused information gathering. Students interested in programs geared toward particular disabilities (e.g., ADD) should investigate the training and certification of any "coaches" whose services are included in Level III programs or whose services may require an extra fee.

In addition to researching the individual background of staff members who provide support, students should get additional specific information on the services offered:

✓ Is there one-on-one tutoring? If so, who does the tutoring? What is that person's educational/professional background?

✓ How often can students meet with someone? Does this number of meetings per week decrease from year to year?

✓ Are additional sessions available for an extra fee?

✓ If the program (or college) offers courses like Study Skills, can students earn credit for these?

✓ Is there special academic advising available?

One of the most important things students can do when they research Level III programs is to compare these fee-for-service programs to the Level I (and Level II, if available) services the college provides. Students might find that they would be paying for a program but not receiving much more in the way of help and accommodations than students who utilize regular (i.e., free) services and accommodations.

have somehow managed to secure an assurance of this from DS ahead of time; instead, the safest bet is for students to choose a college whose graduation requirements are realistic for them (see box, "A Word About Graduation Requirements" on page 105).

Visiting Colleges

Campus visits can help to expand students' preliminary research. Students can locate information on organized college tours and information through the "prospective students" link on a college's main web page. In addition to observing the college's schedule for group information sessions, it is important for students to call or e-mail any department or program contacts before visiting in order to make sure that an office will be open (especially for weekend or summer visits). Similarly, students should set up an appointment with DS staff to further discuss the college's support program, rather than "drop in" while visiting the campus. This type of preparation also provides an opportunity to practice self-advocacy (see Step 2; Banerjee & Brinckerhoff, 2009). YoUniversityTV has created over 500 virtual college tours, and also offers "a day in the life" videos of a variety of careers:

                                                    www.youniversitytv.com/

Visiting the DS Office

The traditional campus tour is unlikely to include DS, and the students who run campus tours are unlikely to be able to answer any questions about DS (unless, by chance, they utilize the office's services—and they may be reluctant to talk about it in such a setting). Students who want to visit DS in order to gather more information should be sure to

---

What Does Admissions Know?

Students should be cautious about asking representatives from the Admissions Office about disability accommodations and services. It's not that these representatives will take notes about their conversation and later make sure the student is denied admission to the college. Rather, it is because these representatives are unlikely to know much (if anything) about the college's policies regarding accommodations and course substitutions or waivers. "Jane" found out the hard way. She has dyslexia and a central auditory processing disorder, and when she was visiting schools during her college search, she asked an admissions representative at the college she now attends about the possibility of a foreign language exemption. Though the representative said that there wouldn't be a problem, it took Jane two years to get her college to agree to a substitution. But it still hasn't been easy for Jane. Her school agreed that she could take American Sign Language as a substitution, but her college doesn't offer it, and Jane was not allowed to take it at the nearby school for the deaf because her college does not consider that class to be at the college level. She is still seeking a solution that will satisfy her school.

call ahead or make an appointment to make sure that the staff member(s) who will be in the office will be knowledgeable about the college's support services.

In visiting the DS office, it is somewhat appropriate to "judge a book by its cover":

- Is the DS office in a cramped space in a leaky basement, or in a location that is inaccessible to students with mobility impairments? This may indicate how much the college values the services that the office provides.

- Is the office full of new adaptive technology equipment, study spaces, and other accommodations that are helpful to students? This also speaks volumes about the college's commitment to helping students with disabilities. Some offices may be in need of a paint job (many schools have experienced budget cuts over the past few years), but if they seem well appointed with items designed to help students, take this as a positive sign.

In preparing for the DS visit, it's helpful to compile a list of questions in advance (see Table 6-3 on pages 123-124); smartphones are great for making sure that the list goes with the student!), and to compile information on the student's educational supports history and disability (see Step 7 for more on documentation). Students need to be comfortable discussing their disability with DS. It can be helpful to role-play or stage a practice "DS visit" in preparation, or to develop

A Word About Graduation Requirements

Because colleges are not required to make changes to their essential requirements, it is incumbent upon students to do their college research carefully, making sure that they can meet both the admission and the graduation requirements at the colleges they are considering (Madaus, 2009).

Programs that require internships or field experiences generally also have a set of requirements for these programs. Frequently, as discussed in Step 1, the main consideration in decisions about accommodations for field experiences is the safety of students and others with whom they work—but even experiences that do not cover health and safety may have requirements that can't be altered without creating a "fundamental" change. Students unable to complete the field experiences required for their major without accommodations deemed unreasonable may be considered not otherwise qualified to complete a degree in that field. Again, this is why the choice of a major is so important, and students have to do their research into the technical requirements carefully (Madaus, 2009). DS may already have worked with a student in students' chosen field and may have arranged some creative accommodations that students might not have considered, so it is definitely worthwhile to ask DS about such ideas. But students also need to be prepared for the idea that some accommodations may not be negotiable.

a "cheat sheet" summarizing pertinent information about the disability and accommodations desired (see Table 6-4 on pages 125-126).

DS staff might be willing to suggest what would be considered appropriate accommodations based on this discussion, or to review the student's documentation with an eye toward what accommodations might be available (see Step 5). In requesting this review, students should stress to DS staff that they understand that having this discussion does not mean a promise of services; rather, the request is intended to establish whether the college offers the best fit for their disability-related needs. Even if the DS staff initially refuses such a request, they may be willing to do such a review later, after students are admitted, to help them make an educated decision about which colleges' services are the best match for them.

It may become clear during the DS visit that the student's desired accommodations are not available at that school—or may not be offered based on the student's profile—or that the college is not a good match for the student because of the level of support being sought. This can be hard to hear, especially if the school is a student's favorite. But it is important to be realistic about the student's need for accommodation and the school's ability or willingness to provide the requested supports. It is up to students to decide how much of a role accommodations will play in their success at college.

The Parents' Role in College Visits

College tours offer students another opportunity to exercise their self-determination and self-advocacy skills. Students need to be comfortable asking questions of administrators and authority figures on their own, as this is what they will be doing at college. Parents should play a supporting but not directing role on these trips (Banerjee & Brinckerhoff, 2009). In addition, "most disability support service directors/coordinators prefer to meet individually with the student without parent prompting in order to get an accurate reading of the student's level of motivation, social skills, and self-knowledge" (Banerjee & Brinckerhoff, 2009, p. 250).

So, if they attend, parents should make it clear that their purpose is to observe—not to answer questions—unless the DS director addresses parents directly (see box, "DS and the Parent Connection" on page 107). Of course, parents may have their own questions, which absolutely should be answered while they are on campus; however, like their students, they need to plan ahead. If they have many questions, they should contact the DS office separately to ask whether they need to make their own appointment, or whether the student's appointment block will allow for such a conversation. (Parents may be asked to submit their questions by e-mail if the DS director's schedule is very busy, which it frequently is.) If they have only a question or two, these can be raised after the student's questions have been answered. The priority is for DS to talk to the student, not the parents. Jane Jarrow, a renowned authority on postsecondary disability services, understands parents' concerns: she sent her daughter, who has cerebral palsy, off to college a few years ago. Jarrow's "Open Letter to Parents" offers sympathy, information, and advice for how to handle students' college visits at:

www.ahead.org/affiliates/kentucky/letter_to_parents

   Parents can help students by discussing their own impressions from college tours and DS visits. It can be productive to compare responses and impressions, particularly in identifying the student's anticipated need for accommodations at college and their availability. Such discussions might lead to suspending certain accommodations in the high school setting (see Step 5), to test whether students can perform effectively on their own. If students' grades do not suffer tremendously, and the student's

---

DS and the Parent Connection

   Parents have much good information to offer about their son or daughter, which we in DS are eager to have. During meetings with interested students and parents, we want to hear what parents can tell us about their students, but we also have an interest in helping parents and students understand students' rights and responsibilities so that they get a good sense of what students need to do prior to, and after, their arrival on campus in order to access services. It is unfortunate, however, that many times the expectations of disability services are vastly different from the realm of what is actually provided as an accommodation.

   Mikael Snitker, Assistant Professor and Rehabilitation Counselor,
   Ferris State University, Michigan

   I went up to the front desk for my next appointment and invited E., a prospective student, back to my office. She got up and her mother, father, and younger brother followed me back to my office. The family was arranged in a semi-circle opposite me with E. on one end of the arc and her father on the other. I turned to E. and asked her how I could help her. Before she could answer her father began with, "My daughter has a learning disability impacting her reading, processing speed and writing." At his pause for a breath I turned to E. and asked, "Can you tell me how your learning disability influences your approach to classes, tests and assignments?" Dad answered, "She gets extra time, separate testing, tutoring, books on tape, spelling is not counted against her on tests and she gets to rewrite papers after feedback. We need to make sure you can arrange these services here." Once again I turned to E. when Dad paused for a breath and asked if she could tell me about how each of these accommodations worked in different classes. For the third time, Dad began to respond, but this time E. turned to her father and said "Shut up! There are things I need to find out here." There was a stunned silence from the father and a shocked look on Mom's face and a snicker from her brother. After a few moments I said to E., "It is clear that you are going to graduate. Let's talk about how."

   She did come to the college where I was working at the time and earned her BA and Master's degree in Special Education.

   L. Scott Lissner, ADA Coordinator, Ohio State University

confidence improves as a result of being able to work without extensive accommodations, then a college that doesn't offer a high level of services might be appropriate.

Parents have a role to play in helping students to prepare for and conduct their college search, and in providing support—but they should not do the research for students. Seeking out information, asking questions, and evaluating the answers they receive are all skills students need to be successful in college, and the college search is a very appropriate place for them to practice these skills (Banerjee & Brinckerhoff, 2009; Shaw, 2009). Going to College provides resources and planning for college, including self-assessment, campus life, and preparing for and applying to college:

www.going-to-college.org/index.html

The Admissions Process

It is easy to understand why some families believe that there is a separate "gate" for admissions for students with disabilities: They may be accustomed to having had a lot of barriers removed for students during the preceding years. However, with the exception of colleges that have special programs for students with disabilities (for which there is typically an additional charge), most schools hold all prospective students to the same standards. So, if Hamblet University requires a 4.0 grade point average (GPA), a cumulative SAT score of over 2000, and 100 extracurricular activities, it does not have to make any modifications to these requirements for students with disabilities.

Colleges that have special fee-for-service programs for students with disabilities may have different admissions requirements for students applying to these special programs, and students may be instructed to send their whole application packet to that program for consideration. But most schools require students to be admitted to the university through standard procedures and then apply, postadmission, for accommodations or admission to the special program. If students get accepted to the university but not to the special program, their rejection for the special services program does not have any effect on their acceptance to the university; they just have to decide whether they want to attend the college without access to the special program.

It is against the law for colleges to inquire about student disabilities during the admissions process. (An exception to this rule applies in a very specific circumstance where a college has been found to be discriminating against students with disabilities; these schools may make such inquiries for the purpose of increasing their admission of such students, but students have to be informed that it is up to them whether or not they wish to identify themselves during the admissions process.) So, when students apply to any school, disclosure of their disability is completely voluntary. Their SAT or ACT reports will not indicate whether they received testing accommodations, and students' high school transcripts will not indicate that they have had an individualized education program (IEP) or Section 504 plan (see box, "To Disclose or Not to Disclose?" on page 109).

To Disclose or Not to Disclose?

At the college level, the choice to identify themselves and ask for services is totally up to students. Students may resist applying for services for a variety of reasons. One frequently cited reason is that they are tired of being different from their classmates; students say that they want to be like everyone else (Barnard-Brak, Lechtenberger, & Lan, 2010; Marshak et al., 2010). What these students don't realize is that they actually are like many of their fellow college students. A recent U.S. government report stated that roughly 11% of students at college have a disability (U.S. Government Accountability Office, 2009). So, in a class of 20 people, there will be at least one other person who has self-identified (and likely more with disabilities who have not asked for services).

Still, some students with disabilities do not self-identify and request services because they want to shed their identify as a person with a disability (Marshak et al., 2010); they see college as a fresh start and wish to exclude their disability from their new image. Though they might not be swayed by the information, students should be told that registering with DS and requesting services does not mean that they will be placed in classes separate from their classmates or that they will be required to attend special instructional sessions.

Another reason that students do not self-identify is that they want to be perceived as being as capable as their classmates, and they are afraid professors and staff members will have a negative impression of them (Barnard-Brak et al., 2010; Marshak et al., 2010). Students whose disability may become fairly obvious with the first class or two (e.g., a student with a noticeable verbal tic) might find it a little more comfortable for themselves and their professors if their professors have a cogent explanation for certain movements or observable behaviors. Those concerned about negative perceptions of their abilities should remember that the best way to counteract any negative perceptions is to demonstrate their skills through classwork and participation.

Other students with disabilities worry about their classmates' perceptions (Barnard-Brak et al., 2010; Marshak et al., 2010). The fact is that, except in cases where students take their exams outside of the regular exam room, their classmates are unlikely to even know that they are getting accommodations, and—frankly—many are unlikely to care. This generation of students is accustomed to seeing different things happen for different classmates with disabilities; it has become part of the normal school experience, so they are unlikely to even notice. Most college students are much more concerned about how they themselves are doing than whether or not their classmate gets audio books.

Still other students are concerned about fairness (Marshak et al., 2010), and think that having adjustments like extra time for exams might give them an advantage over their classmates. These students should remember that disability laws were enacted to level the playing field; accommodations in the college setting provide them with **equal access** to the curriculum. In the case of extended time on exams, it's the difference between having the luxury of a little extra time to polish one's essay (for the student who doesn't need an accommodation) and being able to complete the test at all (for the student who does).

The prohibition on preadmissions disability inquiries is a relief to some students, but not to all. Some students think that their disability is an important part of who they are, or they are proud of the work they have done to overcome the challenges of their disability, and they want to discuss this in their application. But will disclosing their disability on their application or in their essay hurt their chances for admission? The application is students' only chance to show a college who they are, why they would be an asset, and why they think they will succeed. Will disclosing a disability help the college to evaluate the application? What if the person reviewing applications doesn't have an evolved understanding of disabilities?

College Admissions Q&A

The college search and application process can raise questions for all students, but students with disabilities may have even more considerations in choosing which schools to apply to and in deciding how much to reveal in the application process. In this Q&A, seven professionals who work advising students during their college search offer their thoughts on questions that students with disabilities frequently ask about looking at colleges and applying to them.

Ginger Fay (GF), Director of Fay College Counseling, was an admissions officer at Duke University, and has worked in college admissions and counseling for over 15 years.

Steve LeMenager (SL) served as Director of Admission at Princeton University for many years and is currently President of Edvice, an international educational consulting firm based in Princeton and London.

David Flink (DF), who has dyslexia, is a former Admissions Officer at Brown University, where he earned his undergraduate degree and where he served as the office's liaison for students with disabilities. He is Executive Director and Co-Founder of Project Eye-To-Eye, an organization that connects elementary students with disabilities with older mentors who also have disabilities, and he uses his experience to help guide these students as they complete their college applications.

Sarah Estes Merrell (SM) is a high school college Counselor and former college DS Director who has learning disabilities and considered many of these issues during her own college search.

Carolyn Mulligan (CM) is the mother of two students with disabilities whom she helped with their college applications before she became a professional college advisor.

Ann Nault (AN) is a school Counselor at a public high school who helps students with their college search and who has a special interest in helping students with disabilities.

Cally Salzman (CS) is a high school Learning Disabilities Specialist and College Counselor; she previously ran a college DS office.

The advice presented here gives a wide range of views from professionals with many different personal and professional experiences. Students should consider the advice of the counselors with whom they work directly and who know them personally alongside the recommendations of these professionals, who offer additional insights.

Q *My SAT scores are lower than the average score for admitted students at the colleges I am considering. If I tell them that I have a learning disability, will they evaluate me under different criteria?*

> *The discussion about test scores should take into consideration students' application as a whole. Do they have the required courses? Is their GPA in the competitive range for that college?*

SL: Generally speaking, the answer to this question is "no." However, different colleges review students with learning disabilities in different ways. As time goes on, more and more colleges are aware of different learning strengths and challenges and want to determine if they would be the right match for the student. Over the past several years, some colleges have made the submission of SAT or ACT scores optional. I advise students whose scores are low to look at those average scores at each college that interests them and then submit their scores if theirs match or exceed the average. If yours are lower than the average, talk to your school guidance counselor, who may have a good enough sense of the academic and support cultures of each school to guide you on the advisability of submitting your test scores. The discussion about test scores should take into consideration students' application as a whole. Do they have the required courses? Is their GPA in the competitive range for that college? In other words, are all of the other pieces of their application strong? If so, the test scores very well might not work against them.

> *But having scores that exceed the average of those admitted does not mean they will be automatically admitted, just as having scores below the middle 50% range does not mean a student cannot be admitted.*

GF: Most colleges publish either an average score or the middle 50% range of admitted students' scores; these statistics are helpful for students considering applying to a given college. Once they have established their own criteria, students should apply to a range of schools that meet their academic and personal criteria—from those likely to admit them to those that are more of a reach. But having scores that exceed the average of those admitted does not mean they will be automatically admitted, just as having scores below the middle 50% range does not mean a student cannot be admitted.

Second, a number of colleges, including both those that practice "automatic admission" (based on a combination of quantifiable criteria like grades and standardized test scores) and those that practice "holistic admission" (using both objective and subjective criteria), encourage students who feel that their statistics are not an accurate reflection of their ability and potential to write about that feeling in a separate statement to accompany their applications. This invitation would indicate that these schools are, in fact, evaluating at least some applicants differently, though this opportunity is not exclusively available to students with learning disabilities and they are not being evaluated differently simply because they have a disability. Third, an increasing number of schools are practicing test-optional admissions, meaning that students are not required to submit standardized test scores or can submit an alternative set of scores or graded assignments in place of the SAT or ACT. The website of the National Center for Fair & Open Testing maintains an accurate, up-to-date list of test-optional schools:

www.fairtest.org/

The SAT is just small piece of a holistic picture.

CS: Here in California, our state colleges rely heavily on scores. At private colleges, I think it depends upon how the rest of the evaluation looks. The SAT is just small piece of a holistic picture. I think it also depends upon who works in the admissions office. When I worked as a learning disabilities specialist at a university, Admissions staff members would ask me questions in situations where students had voluntarily disclosed their disability in some way on their application. They wanted to know more about what the information meant in order to complete the picture of who these students were.

Colleges do not want excuses for why students may not have done well, but they want explanations, and if something will show them more about a student's profile, they like to know it—

CM: It varies from college to college. Some say that they do not want to know. But some say that they will work with DS when students choose to disclose and that knowing about a disability helps them because this information explains part of who the total student is. One state university admissions representative says that colleges do not want excuses for why students may not have done well, but they want explanations, and if something will show them more about a student's profile, they like to know it. The admissions office members might not look at the disability documentation themselves, but send it to DS for a knowledgeable read on it.

> *Own this process and make sure that the application ultimately speaks to you as a student even if that means writing some optional essays!*

AN: It is my understanding that most colleges will not evaluate students with disabilities under separate criteria, but the learning disability can become a piece of the puzzle just like test scores are a piece—not a sole determination of admissibility. It is important to realize that so many schools are going to a holistic review and evaluating on criteria that is more than a test score from a single Saturday. If the student's total record reflects a student that is quite different from the SAT or ACT test score, the value of the test score will not be as important in the final decision. For those colleges and universities that aren't holistic and use a weighted index using cumulative grade point average and the SAT or ACT, the student is usually given an opportunity somewhere on the application to make note of why the test score may not be an accurate reflection of ability or potential. Students need to take these opportunities—if it says in the application that it is optional to add anything more, take the option! Own this process and make sure that the application ultimately speaks to you as a student even if that means writing some optional essays!

SM: If you don't meet the admissions criteria, you're welcome to share a compelling reason as to why you should be considered—but you should also know that this means you are not "otherwise qualified" for admission.

DF: No colleges will say that they have different criteria. What they will say is that they are trying to take in the full scope of the candidate so that they can understand the student better. What they will want to know is how you dealt with it. What tools have you learned to use? What does it mean to you? Maybe you can explain that, for example, although you aren't a good test taker, you're a good writer, and that you plan to apply to the writing program. If students want to say something, they should tell the whole story about their learning so that the college sees a full picture.

Q   *Is it appropriate to make assumptions about colleges' philosophy on the basis of their policy regarding the submission of standardized test scores?*

SL: Students should not use colleges' test-score policy to evaluate whether a school would be a good fit for students with disabilities. Admissions policy can be quite different from academic policy, and a school that requires standardized test scores might be the right match for students because of the way teaching is done at that school. In other words, students should not steer away from applying to colleges that require test scores based on a faulty assumption that this says something about how they treat students with disabilities. Also, there are myriad reasons for a college to decide to become test-optional, including its sense that other factors are more important in their holistic selection process and a general perception that intense standardized testing preparation has diluted the overall value of SAT and ACT.

GF: The over 800 four-year colleges and universities in the United States that have gone (or always have been) test-optional have made that choice because—as the FairTest organization puts it—they believe "test scores do not equal merit." Although students with learning disabilities may be among the groups that benefit from this change in policy, most colleges and universities that made this change did so in an effort to recruit a more diverse and academically capable student body.

> *If a college or university is test-optional, I think it speaks to the overall mission of the school.*

AN: Colleges and universities really understand standardized testing and the role it should play or not play in the admission decision. Admissions officers are not blind to the shortcomings of the SAT or ACT and they are well aware of the predictive value these scores might play in determining the future success of a student on their campus. If a college or university is test-optional, I think it speaks to the overall mission of the school. The decision isn't made to go test-optional to give an advantage to one or more groups of students for whom standardized testing might not be an accurate reflection of potential success but to put this whole college admission process into a healthy perspective.

SM: It is really valuable to talk to the people in DS to get a sense of how the school treats students with disabilities.

> *If you want to find out if a school is a good fit, "look under the hood."*

DF: If you want to find out if a school is a good fit, "look under the hood": Research their disability services rather than their admissions policies, and know yourself as a learner. For instance, Brown and Columbia are two Ivy League schools with supportive disability services and similar admission criteria. Columbia's curriculum has a very structured program, so it is good for students who want to study across several disciplines and complete distribution requirements. Brown's program is student-designed, so students who go there have to be prepared to chart their own course of study. Using these two comparable schools as examples, students can see the importance of knowing what kind of learning environment suits them best.

Q Is it to students' advantage to disclose a disability?

SL: There are some colleges that are interested in having disabilities information disclosed and they do so in trying to garner more information to establish the best match for their schools, not as a way to weed students out of the pool. This is a new development in the field, but is not an across-the-board phenomenon, so relative caution is still strongly suggested. For some students, disclosing their learning disabilities will be an important part of their "story" or narrative. For most, it will not.

> *Although most students will have no reason to disclose their learning disabilities, there are some situations in which it might be appropriate for a student to do so.*

GF: It depends. Although most students will have no reason to disclose their learning disabilities, there are some situations in which it might be appropriate for a student to do so. For example, the transcript of a student whose ADHD was not diagnosed until later in high school might look like Dr. Jekyll and Mr. Hyde's transcript: The first half of high school, the student's grades were erratic at best and then after diagnosis and treatment, the student has made a dramatic turnaround. In such a case, it may be appropriate for the student and/or his or her counselor to address the turnaround within the application.

CS: In situations where disabilities impact students' GPA or test scores, I think that these students should disclose as a way of explaining that impact. Especially if students' disability was a significant part of their academic life, I encourage them to talk about it in their essay.

CM: I encourage my students to disclose, especially if there's a huge discrepancy between GPA and standardized test scores.

AN: It is a part of who the student is and is not cause to be embarrassed or ashamed. I used to say to students that they learned differently but then a colleague corrected me and said that it is a disability when they do

"Why would a student hide this anymore than he or she would hide other aspects about his/her life?"

not learn the way that most others do. There isn't anything wrong with that and it means the student needs to own his/her learning style and be prepared to be his/her own best advocate. Why would a student hide this anymore than he or she would hide other aspects about his/her life?

SM: I think that it can be important to disclose for the integrity of application when it is relevant to students' identity. It can add weight if it is done well—if students do not use their disability as an excuse for weaknesses in their academic performance. It is complicated. I say disclose your heart away; however, a colleague of mine who worked in admissions at an Ivy League school (and who has a learning disability himself) insists that people in admissions just aren't savvy enough to understand nuances. But I still think that students should lay it out, as long as they are comfortable with this piece of their identity.

"What is important is not to use their disability as an excuse, but instead to talk about how they have used this moment to examine their own learning and discuss what they plan to do at college."

DF: I do not think I would say that it is to their advantage or disadvantage to disclose their disability. However, in their essay or in a short-answer attachment, students can explain discrepancies in their scores or performance. What is important is not to use their disability as an excuse, but instead to talk about how they have used this moment to examine their own learning and discuss what they plan to do at college.

Q Should students use the essay to talk about their disability?

"Colleges look to the essay to provide them with insight into who students are beyond the objective credentials detailed in their application."

SL: I do not think it is a good idea. Colleges look to the essay to provide them with insight into who students are beyond the objective credentials detailed in their application. What are their passions? What piece of students' background is not covered in other parts of the application that illuminate facets of their personality? The essay is the chance for students to tell colleges what they think they should know about them. It need not be "a work of art," but it should be authentic and reflect the applicant.

Some students want to write their essay about overcoming their disability, because they think that it would show the colleges that they are persistent, hard-working students. Though such essays would be personal and revealing, I advise against them. My concern is that writing such an essay would label their entire person as "disabled," and students should be viewed as much more than just their disability.

For students who, after hearing such advice, still insist on writing about their disability in their essay, don't write the "obstacle" essay, in which students talk about how hard they have worked at school despite the challenges of their disability. Admissions offices read numerous essays each year from students who have overcome adversity—multiple, severe disabilities; the responsibility of working three full-time jobs while attending high school at night; the death of a parent; battling cancer; and so on. Students who write about overcoming their learning disabilities or ADD are missing an opportunity to discuss something else about themselves. Is spending extra time writing papers and acquiring new study strategies a struggle worthy of special consideration? I do not at all mean to dismiss the efforts of such students as being unworthy of praise, but putting forward this information in an essay that is supposed to be personally revealing runs the risk of being unfavorably compared with essays from other students in the applicant pool who may have a more pronounced disability or come from a severely disadvantaged or tragic situation.

> *I tell students to begin the application process by making two lists: one is a list of all the things they'd like the admissions committee to know about them, the other is a list of the parts of their applications that can help convey these messages.*

GF: I strongly discourage students from writing an essay about their disabilities and how they have overcome them. The essay is the student's one opportunity to speak directly to the admissions committee and that opportunity should not be squandered on information that can and will be shared elsewhere, information that does not distinguish the student from other qualified applicants, or information that seems to be asking the admissions committee to excuse an area of weakness. I tell students to begin the application process by making two lists: one is a list of all the things they'd like the admissions committee to know about them, the other is a list of the parts of their applications that can help convey these messages. Matching items from the two lists—"My math teacher can talk about how hard I work, and my extracurricular list demonstrates my leadership ability"—can help the applicant realize that the essay does not have to do or say it all and actually is most effective when it only has one job to do. In situations where students have worked to overcome something like a learning disability and they wish to include this information but find it difficult to match this information with a part of the application, they can consider writing a separate statement to accompany the application that addresses this issue directly and concisely. This approach would also be appropriate for things like an illness or a family situation that impacted their academic performance.

CS: I advise students to make the disclosure straightforward. Most admissions officers want to know very specific things. What is the disability? Can the student speak articulately about it? What has been the impact of it? How has the student compensated for it? What does he/she plan to do to accommodate or strategize around it in college?

CM: I do not think they should use the long essay, because that is the place to talk about their personality and who they are. At end of the Common Application there is a section that asks if there is anything else students want colleges to know about them. This is a perfect place for a strong personal statement. I encourage students to tell what their disability is and explain the strategies they have used in high school, to show that they can be successful in college using these strategies. Even when colleges do not use the Common Application, they usually ask a similar question, so there is a place for students to disclose. The Common Application is a standardized form used by member institutions; visit:

www.commonapp.org/

for more information.

I encourage students to tell what their disability is and explain the strategies they have used in high school, to show that they can be successful in college using these strategies.

AN: If a student chooses to use this as the topic of his/her essay, I think it is important for the student to frame the essay to say "This is who I am and this is how I've come to know myself as a learner and a scholar. . . This is what I can bring to the community of this campus." It is not enough to say "I have a learning disability" and leave it at that. The student has to be reflective, articulate and knowledgeable about who he/she is.

DF: The most important thing is—whatever topic students choose—to write a good essay. An essay should contain three components: it should exemplify who they are, tell a good story that incorporates aspects of

> *An essay should contain three components: it should exemplify who they are, tell a good story that incorporates aspects of their personality (rather than just providing a list of points describing them), and leave admissions officers wanting more.*

their personality (rather than just providing a list of points describing them), and leave admissions officers wanting more. The essay should show students as individuals ready to take next step to college. Students should make a list of the things they want to say about themselves, then find a way to write about them. Composing an "obstacle" essay means missing an opportunity for students to talk about how they learn. Students with disabilities actually have an advantage here, as they are prepared to talk about how they learn best because they have had to actually think about it. Also, the "obstacle" essay often focuses on the sorrow, not the joy, in students' learning. Is this what they want to convey to admissions officers?

Q *Should students with disabilities be worried about what their teachers might write in their recommendation letters?*

SL: It might be to the student's benefit for teachers to note their academic perseverance in spite of their disability when the students themselves have not made a point of talking about it.

> *If students are concerned about a teacher or counselor writing about your learning differences, ask the recommenders not to address those issues in their letters.*

GF: Students should meet with their teachers and counselors to discuss what they hope the letter of recommendation will address. If students are concerned about a teacher or counselor writing about their learning differences, they should ask the recommenders not to address those issues in their letters. No counselor or teacher should do so without permission from the student and/or his or her family. For students who do want their learning disabilities to be considered as part of the application, it actually is often best for this information to come from a third party such as a teacher or counselor (rather than from the applicant) who can speak objectively about how the student has compensated for these differences. The Family Educational Rights and Privacy Act is generally interpreted as prohibiting school personnel from disclosing a disability without the parents' (or student's, if of legal age) permission: 34 CFR Part 99; 34 CFR §300.610–300.626; visit:

www.wisconsin.edu/gc-off/ deskbook/ferpafaq.htm

for more information.

CM: Students should make sure that they ask for recommendations from teachers who can write a strong positive letter, so that even if their teachers disclose their disability, it will be in a positive context.

SM: I do not think that students need to worry about this. I think many faculty members don't know what to say about students' disability, and they are smart enough not to put something in for fear of saying something they should not.

DF: If students specifically do not want teachers to disclose their disability, they should simply ask the teachers writing the recommendations not to touch on this. The reverse can also be true: Students may ask a teacher to specifically touch on this aspect—how they learn—as it highlights their unique cognitive abilities. Again, focus on the positive.

Having said this, I understand students' concern that people are biased about students with disabilities, and that a person reviewing their file might have such prejudices. Again, if having a disability is a big part of students' identity or it needs to be a part of the application to explain students' whole profile, students should leave it in. If not, they should leave it out and ask the teachers to leave it out as well.

> *I hate to see students embarrassed or hiding. A disability is a part of their lives and if they believe in themselves, they can create a wonderful remarkable life.*

AN: Again, I hate to see students embarrassed or hiding. A disability is a part of their lives and if they believe in themselves, they can create a wonderful remarkable life. I think students should understand that teacher recommendations are to support the student, not take away value. If a student is confident in who he or she is and believes that college will enrich his/her life, then having all of the pieces to the puzzle will be the best way to continue down this path.

Summary

Students should decide for themselves which pieces of advice from the previous discussion best suit their situation and discuss their ideas with their parents and the professionals with whom they work. Students also need to lead the process of gathering the documentation they will need to request accommodations at college. This process will help them to develop their self-advocacy skills and their self-knowledge. Before they graduate, they should make sure that they understand what their documentation says about them and how it supports the requests for accommodation they plan to make at college.

Table 6-2 Disability Service Research Chart (1 of 2)

Disability Services Research Chart (1 of 2)
College
Office Name
DS office phone number
Special program or fees?
If so, program name
DS contact name
Office address on campus

Table 6-2 Disability Service Research Chart (2 of 2)

Disability Services Research Chart (2 of 2)
Assistive technology available?   Yes _____   No _____ Examples?
Common accommodations
Other resources for support
Documentation requirements

Table 6-3 Disability Services Interview Form (1 of 2)

Disability Services Interview Form (1 of 2)
College
Office Name
DS office phone number
DS contact name
Date
Meeting with (name of staff member)
What are the procedures for requesting accommodations and services?
Do most students who apply for services get found eligible?
What are some commonly approved accommodations?

Table 6-3 Disability Services Interview Form (2 of 2)

Disability Services Interview Form (2 of 2)
Do students who are approved for accommodations have to notify professors themselves?
Do students have to make their own arrangements for accommodated testing?
What forms of adaptive technology are available? (Ask to see them.)
Are there special testing rooms or study spaces for students with disabilities? (Ask to see them.)

Table 6-4 Accommodation Request Preparation Form (1 of 2)

Accommodation Request Preparation Form (1 of 2)
Basic Information

My name is:

I'm applying to (name of department or program):

My disability is:

I was diagnosed when I was _____, in the _____ grade.

Some strategies I use on my own to compensate for my disability include:

    1.

    2.

Diagnosis/Documentation

❏   I have testing reports or a medical diagnosis of my disability; my most recent testing or medical report is (date) _____.

❏   I had an IEP or Section 504 plan in high school; my accommodations included:

    1.

    2.

❏   I have other anecdotal support as evidence of my disability (list sources below).

    1.

    2.

Table 6-4 Accommodation Request Preparation Form (2 of 2)

Accommodation Request Preparation Form (2 of 2)
Requested Accommodation

I am requesting:
 	
    1.
 	
    2.
 	
Having this accommodation will help me with:
 	
    1.
 	
    2.
 	
I ☐ have   ☐ have not   used this accommodation before.
 	
(If not used before) I think I will need this accommodation in college because:
 	
    1.
 	
    2.

Alternative Accommodations

What other accommodations does the college offer or approve for students with my disability?
 	
    1.
 	
    2.

Step 7

Put It All Together: Documentation and the Transition Portfolio

The paperwork—testing reports, historical records, and letters—students submit to prove to DS that they have a disability is called documentation. Because it often takes some time to collect the required paperwork, it is a good idea for students to learn what type of documentation their college requires early—as soon as they send in their enrollment deposit. Students need to take an active part in gathering their documentation so that they understand what's in it. They also need to take responsibility for maintaining essential paperwork in their transition portfolio, an evolving collection of information and references to help guide their management of their postsecondary studies.

Step 7

Put It All Together: Documentation and the Transition Portfolio

Before they leave for college, students have to gather together documentation—in the form of historical records, testing reports, and letters—that they will need to support their request for services once they get there. Depending upon students' disability, this documentation will take different forms, but it should establish the presence of a disability and support their request for specific accommodations.

This process of gathering the necessary documentation can help students' self-knowledge (Madaus, 2009); this is why they should be in charge of doing the research to find out what's needed and then gathering the necessary paperwork. But in addition to knowing what paperwork they need, students need to know what this documentation says about them and their learning profile. They have to understand how their test results support their requests, as they may be asked to justify their need for accommodations. They should know what their diagnosis is, and what their specific symptoms are. Such knowledge can be developed throughout students' high school years during discussions about accommodations, but individualized education program (IEP) teams should consider setting up more focused conversations during students' senior year to make sure that they understand (and agree with) the profile outlined by testing, and can explain how the requested accommodations relate to that profile (see Table 6-4, Step 6's "Accommodation Request Preparation Form" on pages 125-126).

What Kind of Documentation Do Students Need to Provide?

The information on what type of documentation a college requires is generally located on the DS page of the college's web site; there typically will be a link to something like "documentation guidelines" or "documentation requirements." Students also can call the DS office if they can't locate this on the web site, or if they have questions about the terminology.

Some schools have a single general set of guidelines, no matter what the disabling condition is; others have separate guidelines for each category (e.g., psychological disabilities). Even when colleges require more information, their requirements typically include certain elements included in more generic guidelines. Table 7-1 on pages 129-130 presents some typical guidelines for documenting accommodated student disabilities.

Table 7-1. Typical College Documentation Guidelines (1 of 2)

Element	Comments
Qualifications of the evaluator	• Colleges may require that psychoeducational evaluation or psychological diagnosis be completed by someone with a Ph.D. • For medical or physical conditions, documentation may have be from a specialist, rather than from a general practitioner, and paperwork from a nurse-practitioner might not be acceptable. • Colleges might request that the professional offering a diagnosis must have specific training or experience in working with adolescents or adults. • Diagnosis done or paperwork completed by a family member or family friend may not be accepted, no matter how qualified the professional is.
Age of documentation	• Some schools require that paperwork or testing be no older than 3 to 5 years (McGuire, 2009). • Colleges may be more flexible about age of testing for nontraditional students (e.g., 5-year-old testing for someone who was 26 at the time of testing) than for students who were in high school or middle school at the time of evaluation. • Even if testing is old, current, objective information contained in the SOP may be sufficient for documentation.
Clinical interview	• Some guidelines may require that evaluators have spoken with student directly (instead of just gathering data from files). • When included in a report, this provides students with a good chance to describe how they experience their disability and to add information about how they function (e.g., how they self-accommodate) that testing results won't show.
History	• Some colleges' guidelines may request students' educational, family, and/or medical history. • Colleges are unlikely to reject paperwork if it doesn't contain a history, though some may for certain disabilities (e.g., for ADD, report may have to show evidence of early problems with attention). • Although a history may not be required, it can be helpful in providing more details about a student's functioning (e.g., a clear pattern of impairment over time and across all kinds of classes) than testing scores alone. • For LD, ASD, and ADD, histories should include descriptive information (e.g., "teachers said he always needed a minute to respond when asked question in class") and objective information (e.g., grades, standardized testing scores, results from previous evaluations). • Might include a description of accommodations students have used in the past and whether or not they have been helpful.

Note. Even if students' documentation is missing some of these elements, they should submit it anyway, as colleges are likely to show flexibility. For instance, colleges understand that, at public schools, school psychologists who do cognitive testing may have a Master's degree instead of a doctorate. They usually don't have a problem with this, and most will try not to send students for additional, expensive evaluations. Students should not pursue new testing or evaluation unless they submit their paperwork and it is rejected. SOP = Summary of Performance; ADD = attention deficit disorder; LD = learning disabilities; ASD = autism spectrum disorder; DSM-IV = Diagnostic and Statistical Manual of Mental Disorders (American Psychiatric Association, 2000).

Table 7-1. Typical College Documentation Guidelines (2 of 2)

Element	Comments
Testing scores	• Applicable in some situations, based on type of disability. • Many colleges require reports to show actual scores for each test administered. • Guidelines may require that, at a minimum, standard scores and percentile ranks be included. • Age or grade equivalents are typically not required by colleges, and they are frequently considered insufficient for documenting a disability if standard scores and percentile ranks are not included.
Clinical summary	• Colleges may request (e.g., for LD and ADD) that evaluators pull together history and current testing results to explain how they have arrived at the diagnosis. • Some guidelines will require summary to rule out other reasons for students' performance (e.g., emotional distress about a romantic breakup causing students' slow performance on tests).
Conclusion or diagnosis	• Some colleges may want the report to provide a specific diagnosis (e.g., "Alex has a disability in the area of visual processing"). • Some colleges may require a diagnostic code from the DSM-IV. • Some colleges may require the summary to offer evidence of a substantial limitation in the area affected by the disability. • Some colleges consider terms such as *mild impairment or learning problem* as indicating that a condition is not substantially limiting, and therefore would probably not find the student eligible for accommodation.
Recommendations for accommodation	• Some colleges' guidelines may require recommendations. • Professionals who do evaluations should try to recommend accommodations appropriate at the college level. • The link between the disability and the recommended accommodations should be explained. • A distinction should be made between school-based accommodations and strategies students should utilize on their own.

Note. Even if students' documentation is missing some of these elements, they should submit it anyway, as colleges are likely to show flexibility. For instance, colleges understand that, at public schools, school psychologists who do cognitive testing may have a Master's degree instead of a doctorate. They usually don't have a problem with this, and most will try not to send students for additional, expensive evaluations. Students should not pursue new testing or evaluation unless they submit their paperwork and it is rejected. SOP = Summary of Performance; ADD = attention deficit disorder; LD = learning disabilities; ASD = autism spectrum disorder; DSM-IV = Diagnostic and Statistical Manual of Mental Disorders (American Psychiatric Association, 2000).

For students with learning disabilities (LD), autism spectrum disorders (ASD), and attention deficit disorders (ADD), colleges often require a psychoeducational evaluation of students' cognitive ability and their academic skills. For medical, psychological, mobility, hearing, and visual conditions, documentation typically must come from a medical professional. Some schools may have checklists for diagnosticians to complete, or they may require doctors to compose a letter containing certain details about students' level of functional impairment (Banerjee & Brinckerhoff, 2009).

Can Students Use Their IEPs or 504 Plans as Documentation?

In a recent study, colleges' responses to a questionnaire indicated that 44% had accepted an individualized education program (IEP) as sole documentation of a learning disability and 40% accepted a Section 504 plan by itself (Raue, Lewis, & Coopersmith, 2011). However, Raue and colleagues (2011) gave no indication as to how detailed these plans were, and whether or not they included testing scores. In contrast, another recent study (Madaus et al., 2010) found that nearly two thirds of the colleges surveyed required results from formal testing. The upshot of this is that students should not rely on their plans to be their sole source of documentation, as many colleges will not find the information they require within these plans (Madaus, 2009). Once they know what their college expects to see in the way of documentation, students should check their IEP or 504 plan to see whether it contains the necessary information.

Where Do Students Get the Required Documentation?

For students with medical, mobility, hearing, psychological, behavioral, and visual disabilities, their entrance to college may be the first time that their diagnosing and/or treating professional has had to provide some sort of paperwork in order to help them document their disability and apply for services. If their college requires their doctor to complete a form, students should print it and send it to the doctor with a copy of the link on the school's web site and contact information for the DS office, in case the doctor has any questions. If colleges require a letter containing certain information, students should print this and also send the link and contact information to their doctor. Students should expect to be in charge of finding out what they need from their doctor; it is not the doctor's responsibility to do this research. However, if doctors have questions about what the university requires, they should be responsible for calling DS, as it will ease communication if they speak directly to someone in the DS office, rather than going through the student. Students with visual or hearing disabilities might have to submit results from standard ophthalmological exams or an audiological evaluation, and some schools require doctors to complete a form in addition to these clinical reports.

For students with other disabilities (e.g., LD, ADD, ASD), colleges generally require pscyhoeducational testing, which evaluates students' cognitive ability and academic skills with standardized, normed tests (see box, "DS and the Professional Connection" on page 134). Most colleges' requirements for this are similar: They require one test battery for cognitive functioning and one test battery for academic functioning (Table 7-2).

What Obstacles Might Students Encounter?

Testing Older Than the Guidelines Allow

Federal law no longer requires high schools to retest students who were identified for special education services in earlier grades, which means that students whose high schools have not evaluated them recently may have some difficulty getting their older documentation accepted at their college (McGuire, 2009). A recent study found that 43% of colleges surveyed required students' testing to be less than 3 years old, and some allowed testing to be up to 5 years old, whereas 33% expressed willingness to look at the documentation age question on a case-by-case basis (Madaus et al., 2010). Students who require more-recent testing have to pay for the testing themselves, as colleges are not required to provide the testing that their documentation standards demand (McGuire, 2009). Because this kind of evaluation can be costly, some colleges may offer testing at reduced rates through a relevant graduate program on campus (e.g., Psychology), or keep a list of outside professionals who do evaluations on a sliding scale. There is a movement in the field to deemphasize currency in order to prevent discrimination on the basis of students' financial resources, but some colleges will hold fast to their requirements about age of documentation, and federal law does not set limits for what colleges can demand. Students who have undergone at least some standardized, norm-referenced testing (e.g., Woodcock-Johnson Tests of Achievement; Woodcock, McGrew, & Mather, 2001a) while they were in high school should have an easier time applying for services once they get admitted to college.

Table 7-2. Tests and Assessments

Cognitive tests	Stanford-Binet Intelligence Scales (Roid, 2004)
	Woodcock-Johnson Tests of Cognitive Ability-III (Woodcock, McGrew, & Mather, 2001b)
	Wechsler Adult Intelligence Scale IV (Wechsler, 2008)
Achievement tests	Wechscler Individual Achievement Test III (Wechsler, 2009)
	Woodcock-Johnson Tests of Achievement-III (Woodcock, McGrew, & Mather, 2001a)
	Nelson-Denny Reading Test (Brown, Vick Fischco, & Hanna, 1993)

Note. Some colleges require students to be tested using adult norms. However, evaluators generally do not use adult test scales when students are in their early high school years. Students tested with the Wechsler Intelligence Scale for Children (Wechsler, 2003) who are enrolling in a college where the documentation requirements mention adult norms should investigate whether their existing test results might be acceptable.

Some colleges do not accept the Wide-Range Achievement test (WRAT-4; Wilkinson & Robertson, 2006) as the sole achievement measure because it only contains three tests and is not sufficiently comprehensive.

Documentation That Does Not Contain the Required Tests

Sometimes students are told that their documentation is insufficient because the college requires certain tests that were not used in their most recent evaluation. Although this doesn't typically happen in the case of students with learning disabilities, it may happen for students with ADD who have only undergone a traditional psychoeducational evaluation or may never have had any kind of testing at all (see box, "ADD and Documentation"). Although high schools are not required to purchase such tests in order to aid students' requests for accommodations at college, they should consider providing the testing students most commonly need to apply for college accommodations, as it will spare those who can least afford it from making the choice between paying for testing or doing without their accommodations at college (see box, "DS and the Professional Connection" on page 134). Students who have never had such testing and whose high schools do not provide it should call DS at the college they plan to attend to see if there are any resources on or off campus to obtain such testing at a reduced cost.

Reported Scores Don't Meet the Requirements

Because high schools conduct testing only for their own purposes (i.e., to see whether students qualify for services), they sometimes report only overall scores (e.g., "full-scale" IQ), or report certain kinds of scores (e.g., grade equivalents). Colleges expect to see all of the scores for any tests given during an evaluation, so students should make sure that these are included in their documentation. Also, colleges may require standard scores and percentile ranks. It's okay if grade or age equivalents are included in students' reports, but they might be considered insufficient in the absence of these other two scores. It's a good idea for someone on the IEP team to explain to students what their testing scores represent.

Before students pursue any additional testing or diagnosis, they should contact the DS office to find out if the documentation they already have will meet the

ADD and Documentation

For years, DS offices have received documentation of ADD in a variety of forms, such as notes from doctors scribbled on a prescription blank saying something like "Elizabeth Hamblet has ADD. Please provide her with whatever accommodations she needs." Sometimes colleges just receive a checklist of symptoms that the student experiences. Clearly, documentation like this does not establish that there is substantial limitation in students' functioning. The absence of a standardized evaluation protocol for ADD has led to the establishment of more stringent requirements by some colleges. Although not actually designed for the purpose of diagnosing ADD, results from psychoeducational testing can help to eliminate (or point to) the presence of a learning disability as the cause of students' inattention and provide quantitative information about how the students function on academic tasks.

college's qualitative and currency guidelines (see box, "Essential Documentation: The Summary of Performance" on page 135). Most schools do try to be reasonably flexible. Many will not send students for extensive, expensive testing unless what students have is very outdated, or is far afield of what is required (e.g., evaluations performed by family members or friends of the family are universally considered a no-no, no matter how qualified the evaluator is). Students who do need to go for testing should know exactly what their college requires and make sure that the professional who will be evaluating them has the required tests. Like medical doctors, psychologists and neurospsychologists are not responsible for knowing what each student needs to apply for services at college; it is students' responsibility to make sure they get what they need.

The emphasis throughout this book is on raising students' awareness of themselves—their strengths and weaknesses, the amount of help they need, their ability to self-advocate, and so forth, throughout high school. Although students don't actually need their documentation paperwork until they are ready to go to college, the kinds of information these documents convey should be familiar to students throughout their high school years, long before they're ready to leave for college. Instead of waiting until second semester of students' senior year to engage them in the documentation gathering process and its attendant discussions, it is much better to have students become familiar with the paperwork—and what it means—over the course of their high school education. The development of a "transition portfolio" is a great method to educate students about themselves and what they will need to apply for services at college.

The Transition Portfolio: Documentation and More

Effective transition planning requires students to start thinking about what they need to be successful at college just as they are entering high school. For many students, such a far-away goal may seem vague and amorphous. One way to keep them focused is to provide a regular review of their progress toward their postsecondary goal of attending college.

DS and the Professional Connection

Professionals who do evaluations should familiarize themselves with the kinds of testing and narrative information colleges require. Professionals can review the documentation requirements of several nearby colleges, or call a few of the DS offices to ask whether certain accommodations that they are in the habit of recommending are commonly approved. They can use this conversation to ask what kinds of adjustments students may easily get at these schools, so they have a realistic idea of what is considered appropriate at the college level. Although evaluators are under no obligation to only recommend accommodations that students can get at the postsecondary level, if they're knowledgeable about postsecondary supports they can at least give students some indication that some of the recommendations they have made may not be available at college.

Banerjee and Brinckerhoff (2009) recommended that, throughout students' years in high school, they collect needed information in a "transition portfolio" (p. 238; Dukes, 2009, also encouraged the development of such a collection). Putting together a compendium of documents will not only make the process of collecting needed information for accommodation requests at college easier and less stressful, but it may also serve as a tangible reminder of the long-term goal, and as a physical embodiment of students' progress.

Initially, the contents of the portfolio might be determined by school professionals and the student's parents. The portfolio should be reviewed an annual basis (perhaps at the annual IEP meeting) or more frequently to make sure that information is regularly being added. As a way of developing their self-determination skills, students should think about what documents should be included that aren't on the list. It is important to review the items in the portfolio—not just quantitatively (i.e., to make sure that IEPs, transcripts, etc., are in there) but qualitatively: What does the information demonstrate about the student's progress toward identified postsecondary goals (Dukes, 2009)? Portfolios should be able to show that students are progressing toward using accommodations appropriate in the college setting (Dukes, 2009) and developing the skills (academic, social, and interpersonal) that will help them to be successful there (Dukes, 2009).

The transition portfolio is for students to use in getting ready for college. It should both serve to help them collect the paperwork they will need and provide an opportunity to reflect on their goals at regular intervals. Once they get to college, they should not expect to simply hand the portfolio over to DS. Instead, they will only take with them the documents they know they need to make accommodation requests and to support these requests.

Table 7-3 on pages 137-139 provides a checklist of items student should collect to help them more effectively self-advocate at college, along with cross-references to the Steps in this book that describe the information. The table can be used both as a checklist and to reference pertinent information throughout the book.

Essential Documentation: The Summary of Performance

The answer to both the currency and the test problem may be found in a document called the Summary of Performance (SOP). High schools are required to provide graduating students who have had an IEP with this document (McGuire, 2009). In developing the SOP, the IEP team should review the documentation guidelines of several colleges (a mix of public, private, 4-year, and 2-year schools) to get a sense of what kinds of information postsecondary institutions want to see. The purpose of the SOP is to help professionals at students' next destination (e.g., college, the workplace) make appropriate accommodations for them. In order to make them helpful to students applying for services at college, SOPs should include both objective (e.g., test scores) and narrative information to provide colleges with a clear picture of students' current level of functioning.

The intent of the transition portfolio is to provide a historical record of the student's academic background and documentation of his or her disability. In addition to materials that help document the student's needs and support any request for accommodation, college-going students should collect in their transition portfolio information specific to the college, such as notes on the services offered by tutoring centers, health services, and so on. The transition portfolio isn't static, though; it should be an evolving collection. While students are in high school, each year's new IEP and transcripts will replace the old ones. Students will not need to take all of the documents that have been included throughout high school when they go to college; they just need the ones required to apply for services. Once students get to college, they can use the portfolio as a way of organizing information relating to disability services throughout college (e.g., a copy of the current semester's Letter of Accommodation, any new testing or medical information, information on the grievance process, transcript, etc.). If they decide to apply to graduate school, some of these documents will likely come in handy when they apply for accommodations at that next level of their education.

Summary

Although the collection of documentation can wait until students' senior year, the development of a transition portfolio over students' high school years is an ideal way to provide natural opportunities to evaluate students' progress toward postsecondary goals while also compiling the necessary documents. Once students decide where they plan to enroll, the emphasis should be on their checking their college's documentation requirements before they finish high school. This way, they can make sure they have easy access to any documents they will need (before school professionals break for the summer).

Throughout this and the other parts of the transition process, adults will assist students by helping them to develop the skills they will need for success and by educating about the legal and academic requirements of the college environment. But what students want to know about college—what it's really like to be a student at college with a disability—is not likely to be found in the information provided by parents and professionals, who may not have been college students with disabilities themselves. This is why it is helpful to share the experiences of students just like them who are enrolled in or have finished college—as the Epilogue to this book does.

Table 7-3. Transition Portfolio Checklist (1 of 3)

Portfolio item	Comments	See...	For student's reference	Submit to college
High school history/background				
Psychoeducational testing and/or formalized norm-referenced testing	• Students should know what testing says about them and be able to explain this when they get to college. • Students should make sure testing results show necessary scores and include required tests needed to apply for services at the college they want to attend.	Step 7, Table 7-1, Typical College Documentation Guidelines (p. 130). Step 7, Table 7-2, Tests and Assessments (p. 132).		✓
Learning styles assessment	• Learning styles assessment tools can be helpful to give students knowledge of their strengths and challenges.	Step 3	✓	
Most recent IEP or Section 504 plan	• Should be checked during annual review to see whether goals and accommodations move students toward independence they will need to be successful at college.	Steps 3 and 4	✓	✓
Summary of Performance	• Probably won't be ready until student graduates. • Should provide results from any evaluations as well as grades, teacher comments on students' performance, etc.	Step 7, Student Summary of Performance samples (pp. 140-144).		✓
Medical records	• Students may need to tell treating professionals what kind of information they will need in order to request accommodations at college.	Step 6		✓
High school transcript	• At the end of each academic year, retain only the most current transcript (rather than individual semester or term grade reports).		✓	

Table 7-3. Transition Portfolio Checklist (2 of 3)

Portfolio item	Comments	See...	For student's reference	Submit to college
College entrance exam (SAT, ACT) information	• Students should retain copies of both their score reports and any approval for testing accommodations granted by the testing agency.		✓	
List of accommodations used in high school	• This list should evolve and shorten each year as students prepare for the college environment.	Step 4	✓	
Resumé	• Compiling information on work experiences, extracurricular activities, volunteer/community service, awards, artistic achievements, etc. throughout high school can help in completing admission applications. • This information (with dates of service) may also help during college, when applying for work, internships, or field experiences.		✓	
College research				
Desired accommodations	• Accommodations must be linked to the student's area of weakness; the student must understand them, think they are helpful, and be able to explain why they are needed.	Step 6, Table 6-4, Accommodations Request Preparation Form (pp. 125-126)		✓
Colleges' disability services documentation requirements	• Students should ask questions of their IEP team if they don't understand the requirements or aren't sure that they have what is required in their portfolio.	Step 6, Table 6-2, Disability Services Research Chart (pp. 121-122). Step 6, Table 6-3, Interview Form (pp. 123–124). Step 6, Table 6-4, Accommodation Request Preparation Form (pp. 125-126).	✓	

Table 7-3. Transition Portfolio Checklist (3 of 3)

Portfolio item	Comments	See...	For student's reference	Submit to college
Colleges' graduation requirements	• This information should be gathered during students' junior year, while they are doing their college research.	Steps 1, 3, 6	✓	
Campus resources (contact information, location, services available)				
Disability services	• This information should be gathered as part of students' college research.	Step 6 Disability Services Research Chart (pp. 121-122)	✓	
Academic support/ tutoring center	• What kinds of services are provided? • Is tutoring done one-on-one or in small groups? • Who does the tutoring? • Are study groups available?	Steps 4, 5, 6	✓	
Health services	• Does the campus Health Services center provide refills for students who take medication? • If not, can they point students to pharmacies that are close to campus? • Do they provide any other services (e.g., injections, coordinating with the counseling center when students need new medications)?		✓	
Counseling center	• Is therapy provided by graduate students (who may change from semester to semester)? • If so, can the center refer students to a local professional near campus? • Is there a limit to how many visits a student can make in a week?		✓	

Student Summary of Performance
Model Template Instructions

Part 1: Background Information – Complete this section as specified. Please note this section also requests that you attach copies of the most recent formal and informal assessment reports that document the student's disability or functional limitations and provide information to assist in post-high school planning.

Part 2: Student's Postsecondary Goals – These goals should indicate the post-school environment(s) the student intends to transition to upon completion of high school.

Part 3: Summary of Performance – This section includes three critical areas: Academic, Cognitive and Functional levels of performance. Next to each specified area, please complete the student's present level of performance and the accommodations, modifications and assistive technology that were essential in high school to assist the student in achieving progress. Please leave blank any section that is not applicable.

An Accommodation is defined as a support or service that is provided to help a student fully access the general education curriculum or subject matter. Students with impaired spelling or handwriting skills, for example, may be accommodated by a note-taker or permission to take class notes on a laptop computer. An accommodation does not change the content of what is being taught or the expectation that the student meet a performance standard applied for all students. A Modification is defined as a change to the general education curriculum or other material being taught, which alters the standards or expectations for students with disabilities. Instruction can be modified so that the material is presented differently and/or the expectations of what the student will master are changed. Modifications are not allowed in most postsecondary education environments. Assistive Technology is defined as any device that helps a student with a disability function in a given environment, but does not limit the device to expensive or "high-tech" options. Assistive technology can also include simple devices such as laminated pictures for communication, removable highlighter tapes, Velcro and other "low-tech" devices.

The completion of this section may require the input from a number of school personnel including the special education teacher, regular education teacher, school psychologist or related services personnel. It is recommended, however, that one individual from the IEP Team be responsible for gathering and organizing the information required on the SOP.

Part 4: Recommendations to assist the student in meeting postsecondary goals – This section should present suggestions for accommodations, adaptive devices, assistive services, compensatory strategies, and/or collateral support services, to enhance access in a post-high school environment, including higher education, training, employment, independent living and/or community participation.

Part 5: Student Input (Highly Recommended). It is highly recommended that this section be completed and that the student provide information related to this Summary of Performance. The student's contribution can help (a) secondary professionals complete the summary, (b) the student to better understand the impact of his/her disability on academic and functional performance in the postsecondary setting, (c) postsecondary personnel to more clearly understand the student's strengths and the impact of the disability on this student. This section may be filled out independently by the student or completed with the student through an interview.

This Student Summary of Performance model template was developed by the National Transition Documentation Summit © 2005 based on the initial work of Stan Shaw, Carol Kochhar-Bryant, Margo Izzo, Ken Benedict, and David Parker. It reflects the contributions and suggestions of numerous stakeholders in professional organizations, school districts and universities particularly the Connecticut Interagency Transition Task Force. It is available to be freely copied or adapted for educational purposes. The model template has been formally ratified by the Council for Exceptional Children's Division on Career Development and Transition (DCDT), Division on Learning Disabilities (DLD), and Council on Educational Diagnostic Services (CEDS), Learning Disability Association (LDA), the Higher Education Consortium for Special Education (HECSE), and the Council for Learning Disabilities (CLD). It is available to be freely copied or adapted for educational purposes.

Student Summary of Performance (1 of 2)

Part 1: Background Information

Student Name: _____ Date of Birth: _____

Year of Graduation/Exit: _____

Address: _____
(Street)   (Town, State)   (Zip code)

Telephone Number: _____ Primary Language: _____

Current School: _____ City: _____

Student's primary disability (Diagnosis): _____

Student's secondary disability (Diagnosis), if applicable: _____

When was the student's disability (or disabilities) formally diagnosed? _____

_____

If English is not the student's primary language, what services were provided for this student as an English language learner?

_____

Date of most recent IEP or most recent 504 plan: _____

Date this Summary was completed: _____

This form was completed by: Name: _____

Title: _____

School: _____

E-mail: _____ Telephone Number: _____

Please check and include the most recent copy of assessment reports that you are attaching that diagnose and clearly identify the student's disability or functional limitations and/or that will assist in postsecondary planning:

☐ Psychological/cognitive   ☐ Response to Intervention (RTI)

Student Summary of Performance (2 of 2)

Part 1: Background Information (cont'd)

Please check and include the most recent copy of assessment reports that you are attaching that diagnose and clearly identify the student's disability or functional limitations and/or that will assist in postsecondary planning:

☐ Psychological/cognitive   ☐ Response to Intervention (RTI)

☐ Neuropsychological   ☐ Language proficiency assessments

☐ Medical/physical   ☐ Reading assessments

☐ Achievement/academics   ☐ Communication

☐ Adaptive behavior   ☐ Behavioral analysis

☐ Social/interpersonal skills   ☐ Classroom observations (or in other settings)

☐ Community-based assessment   ☐ Career/vocational or transition assessment

Part 2 – Student's Postsecondary Goal(s)

1. _____

2. _____

3. _____

If employment is the primary goal, the top three job interests:

_____

_____

_____

Part 3 – Summary of Performance (Complete all that are relevant to the student).

ACADEMIC CONTENT AREA	Present Level of Performance (grade level, standard scores, strengths, needs)	Essential accommodations, assistive technology, or modifications utilized in high school, and why needed.
Reading (Basic reading/decoding; reading comprehension; reading speed)		
Math (Calculation skills, algebraic problem solving; quantitative reasoning)		
Language (written expression, speaking, spelling)		
Learning skills (class participation, note taking, keyboarding, organization, homework management, time management, study skills, test-taking skills)		
COGNITIVE AREAS	Present Level of Performance (grade level, standard scores, strengths, needs)	Essential accommodations, assistive technology, or modifications utilized in high school, and why needed.
General Ability and Problem Solving (reasoning/processing)		
Attention and Executive Functioning (energy level, sustained attention, memory functions, processing speed, impulse control, activity level)		
Communication (speech/ language, assisted communication)		

Part 3 – Summary of Performance (Complete all that are relevant to the student).

FUNCTIONAL AREAS	Present Level of Performance (grade level, standard scores, strengths, needs)	Essential accommodations, assistive technology, or modifications utilized in high school, and why needed.
Social Skills and Behavior (Interactions with teachers/peers, level of initiation in asking for assistance, responsiveness to services and accommodations, degree of involvement in extracurricular activities, confidence and persistence as a learner)		
Independent Living Skills (Self-care, leisure skills, personal safety, transportation, banking, budgeting)		
Environmental Access/Mobility (assistive technology, mobility, transportation)		
Self-Determination/Self-Advocacy Skills (Ability to identify and articulate postsecondary goals, learning strengths and needs)		
Career-Vocational/Transition		
Employment (Career interests, career exploration, job training, employment experiences and supports)		
Additional important considerations that can assist in making decisions about disability determination and needed accommodations (e.g., medical problems, family concerns, sleep disturbance)		

Part 4 – Recommendations to assist the student in meeting postsecondary goals

Suggestions for accommodations, adaptive devices, assistive services, compensatory strategies, and/or collateral support services, to enhance access in the following post-high school environments (only complete those relevant to the student's postsecondary goals).

Higher Education or Career-Technical:	
Education:	
Employment:	
Independent living:	
Community participation:	

Part 5 – Student Input (Highly Recommended)

A. How does your disability affect your schoolwork and school activities (such as grades, relationships, assignments, projects, communication, time on tests, mobility, extra-curricular activities)?

B. In the past, what supports have been tried by teachers or by you to help you succeed in school (aids, adaptive equipment, physical accommodations, other services)?

C. Which of these accommodations and supports has worked best for you?

I have reviewed and agree with the content of this Summary of Performance.

Student Signature: _____ Date: _____

Source: http://www.vacollegequest.org/charting/SOPmodelform.pdf

Epilogue

The College Experience

High school students who want to know what college is really like can learn a lot from current college students and recent graduates. These students' real-life experiences provide details about what to expect and advice on how to be successful—and they give younger students hope for their own future. Even experiences that are not always completely positive can help other students by providing the reassurance that they are not alone in their struggles.

Epilogue

The College Experience

What is the secret to success at college? As these stories illustrate, factors that help contribute to students' success are knowledge of their learning style, organization of time and materials, effective study techniques, a willingness to seek help and information, and building and utilizing support networks (see box "DS and the Professional Connection"). None of the students whose stories I relate attributed his or her success to the use of accommodations; instead, all of them have taken responsibility for their own learning, using a proactive approach to their studies.

Sam

A current junior, Sam is diagnosed with dyslexia. His college accommodations include time-and-a-half for in-class exams and the option of using a computer on tests. He typically takes tests in the Learning Resource Center, but sometimes professors want him to take tests in their office.

Sam was fortunate in high school—his parents helped him develop self-advocacy skills. When he needed help at school or had a problem, his mother encouraged him to talk to teachers himself (although sometimes she would e-mail them privately if she thought teachers needed to know something). In his college search, he focused on smaller colleges knowing that, at these schools, professors would have more time to give to him.

DS and the Professional Connection

Reading about students' experiences at college is helpful to students, but first-hand conversations are even better. Christina Cacioppo Bertsch, a former college DS coordinator who specializes in college admissions counseling for students with disabilities, recommends that schools arrange to have their graduates who have made a successful transition to college come back to their high school to talk about what has worked and what has been challenging for them. It can be included as part of a college night where school representatives visit, or set aside as a separate event.

Another idea is for college-bound students to contact the DS at the colleges they will be visiting to see if the office can arrange for them to meet with a student. This is a great way for students to find out how services work and hear what it is like to be a student with a disability on that particular campus.

Perhaps as a result of his high school experience, Sam is very comfortable approaching professors with his questions, which he feels gives him a better sense of what they are looking for in a particular assignment. While in high school, he also learned how organization could help him keep on top of materials and reduce his stress levels.

Even though his disability directly affects his reading, Sam has not allowed it to be an obstacle to him in studying literature. In fact, he says that he cannot imagine what he would be like without his learning disability. Sam says that because he was told that writing was a weakness, he actually worked harder at it to improve his skills. He knows how he learns best and uses systems that work for him. For instance, he uses No Fear Shakespeare to help him understand the original literature's language. Sam uses aids such as Sparknotes, not as substitutes for reading his assignments, but rather to boost his comprehension. No Fear Shakespeare shows students Shakespeare's dialogue side-by-side with modern translations of his words. Visit:

www.nfs.sparknotes.com/

What Works for Sam?

✓   A system for organization. Sam creates folders on his laptop for each class he takes, and then within those folders creates a subfolder for each assignment in which to store notes and drafts.

✓   A calendar to track assignment deadlines and tests. Managing time is one of the most important things students need to learn before they get to college.

✓   Professors' office hours and study groups. Sam utilizes professors' office hours to ask about class content and to show them drafts of papers. He talks to his professors about his disability, and he attends study sessions that teaching assistants offer. Sam acknowledges that some professors are more approachable than others, but "being shy or 'intimidated' by a professor doesn't work anymore. . . the teacher will not seek you out." He thinks interacting with professors is a great way to make sure his notes and work are on track with professors' expectations.

Francis

Francis is currently a sophomore. Although he receives accommodations, he does not know the actual name of his disability. In his college search, Francis didn't focus on the disability services (DS) office; if a school offered services, that was enough for him. At college, Francis uses minimal accommodations similar to those he had in high school: testing with extended time in a separate location from his classmates, where distractions are reduced. These simple adjustments are very helpful, although he is still getting used to being away from home and adjusting to the amount of work he has to do. He notes that college is a very different environment and "it is a process that takes a long time to get used to." But he feels that his use of strategies puts him at an advantage over his peers, who are struggling to adjust to the college setting.

Francis feels that he was well prepared for the college environment: His high school provided him with the information he needed to get accommodations at college, which made his transition smooth, and he developed techniques for studying and time management that have served him well in college. Francis notes that some students he knows who do not have disabilities still have not figured out how to manage their time and do not seem to have the self-discipline to avoid distractions and get down to work.

What Works for Francis?

✓   A lighter course load. Even with his level of organization, when he first started at college Francis was really overwhelmed. Now he knows how many classes he can realistically handle while also maintaining a life outside of his academic work, which is a priority for him.

✓   Knowing what expectations professors have, and understanding what to do to meet them.

✓   A semester-long calendar recording all major projects and papers that need to be completed. This helps Francis to allot the time he needs in order to meet his deadlines. When final exams approach, he writes out the amount of time he will need to study for each subject. In the 2 weeks before exams, he spreads out his study time for each class so that he has sufficient time devoted to each subject and still has time for a break.

Katie

Katie, a recent college graduate, is diagnosed with attention deficit disorder (ADD) and dyslexia. Katie's college search included visits to DS offices and meetings with the directors; her decision about which college to attend was influenced by the facts that the DS director was experienced in working with students with disabilities and that the school offered her access to text-to-speech technology. Katie notes that some of her friends who did not do their college research as carefully as she did ended up at schools where the professors really did not know anything about learning disabilities. Katie's accommodations included extended time for tests, administered in a separate room, the option to use a calculator on tests, and the ability to get copies of notes from a classmate.

Although Katie's parents and high school helped her to get ready, she says, "college is a totally different ball game. . .It's really up to you to do the work. You have to learn as you go." Like so many students with (and without) disabilities, Katie did not manage her time well when she was a freshman. "The grades that I got reflected that I wasn't putting in enough time and I just learned I needed to study more." Katie says she knew that she should have been spending more time studying outside of class, but it took seeing her grades to get her to understand the importance of managing her time and doing more work. After being put on academic probation because of her poor grades, Katie met with an advisor once a week for help with time management. "College is one of those places where you go with a flow and figure things out," Katie says.

What Worked for Katie?

✓ Attending professors' office hours. Students who do this "make a name" for themselves—teachers know them, understand their difficulties, and see their eagerness to do well.

✓ Being organized, especially bringing appropriate materials to each class. When her professors posted notes or slides online, Katie would print them out and bring the printouts to class so she could take additional notes on them.

✓ Not waiting until the last semester to take hard classes.

✓ Seeking support from the college's DS office.

✓ Finding her passion (Katie's is painting—which she discovered in her sophomore year) and having faith that "things will work out the way they are supposed to."

Christi

Christi is diagnosed with attention deficit hyperactivity disorder (ADHD) and mild dyslexia. She did not consider disability services as part of her college search; her focus was on schools that had Division I rowing teams and which seemed realistic given her grades and scores. The only accommodation Christi used in college was extended time for tests.

Before college, Christi attended a supportive private high school where she worked with an extremely helpful counselor whose advice and guidance, Christie says, was invaluable. She felt prepared for college, but once she got there, she thought that "the kids from the East Coast clearly had a better education in K to 8."

Christi's experiences at college were not as positive as those of the other students who shared their stories. It is important to share experiences such as hers so that students whose transition to college is hard know that they are not alone.

A few things contributed to Christi's disappointment with her college experience. One was the quality of the advising she received. Late in her college career, she learned that she was missing a course required for her to graduate. Using her self-advocacy skills, she arranged a meeting with the university's president, asking him to help her figure out how to get the class she needed so that she could graduate with her class (the president found it difficult, too). Christi also found that—at her college—many of the other students were not interested in studying or learning, as she was. She found her classmates' focus on partying disheartening, but she ignored the social distractions and focused on the reasons why she was at college. Even though Christi did not really like her college, she persevered and earned her degree. She is now in a job that she really enjoys.

The transition to college can be hard, so students should not think that there is something wrong with them if they are struggling and feeling unhappy. Many students with and without disabilities struggle to get used to the college environment. Christi views being tested by the college environment as having been a formative experience for her, and she wants students with disabilities to remember that school is just one part of their lives. Christi says that she learned a lot about her strengths while at college; her struggles taught her perseverance, which has served her well in her postcollege life. She says that she is tenacious in learning things, always looking up words or ideas that people use in her field, which puts her far above her peers and gets her recognition at work.

What Worked for Christi?

✓ A schedule to organize her time.

✓ Testing strategies for multiple-choice tests. Christi applied test-taking skills she'd learned when preparing for the SAT—to eliminate the answers she knew were incorrect, and then reread the question and talk herself through the answer.

✓ Focusing on time management to avoid the "crunch" before exams.

✓ Knowing how textbooks operate and using their features, such as review questions, to make sure that she understood and retained information from her reading. Christi recommends doing every optional reading and completing handouts even if professors do not collect them; these assignments make great study tools later.

Nicole

Nicole, a current freshman, is diagnosed with dyslexia and slow information processing. Her college search was different than many students' because she is an athlete who was recruited in her junior year of high school. Even so, disability services did figure into her search; part of her decision to attend her school was influenced by the fact that it had a DS office dedicated just to serving athletes. Nicole's college accommodations are time and a half for in-class exams, a notetaker, and audio books. She plans to ask for double time on exams, as she has not been able to finish some of them because of the amount of writing and complex thinking involved. Nicole takes her exams outside of the classroom, which means she does not have access to her professors to ask questions; as a result, she sometimes misses out on information. (Nicole recently approached a professor after an exam to let her know she had run out of time, and learned that the professor had instructed the class to provide only short answers, not long ones like she had done. Luckily, the professor was very understanding, and considered this in her grading.)

A month before she started college, Nicole and her mother filled a Filofax with information and other useful things, such as a copy of her schedule. Based on her prior experience using a school-supplied agenda book, Nicole doubted that she would get much use out of the Filofax; however, she's found this to be an invaluable resource.

While she was in high school, Nicole used Kurzweil text-to-speech assistive technology and Learning Ally audio books to help her get through reading assignments, techniques that she still uses. Nicole's parents scan textbook pages for her so she can use them with Kurzweil. Kurzweil Education Systems offer "comprehensive reading, writing and learning software"; visit:

www.kurzweiledu.com/default.html

DAISY-format books are available from Learning Ally (formerly Recording for the Blind and Dyslexic):

www.learningally.org/

and on iTunes and as an app;

www.learningally.org/apple/

Although Nicole asked in advance for help in choosing her classes during her college orientation, her advisor did not understand her disability and how it should affect her class choices. As a result, she ended up with two electives, neither of which counts toward the college's distribution requirements or the requirements for her desired major, and one of which required a lot of reading. Nicole finds that many people do not understand her dyslexia, and think it means that she reads backward. Some friends have helped her, sharing notes to make sure that she has not missed anything important in her own notes.

Nicole notes that there is a big difference in the expectations for assignments and tests in college from what she was used to in high school. Papers are more challenging, she says, and there are more parts to them: "You can't just spit out facts—you have to apply facts to different examples and tie them back to your main argument." Nicole notes that this requires a "higher level of thinking, not just memorization. You have to give the connection and apply it."

What Works for Nicole?

✓ Having a notetaker, although the quality of notes varies according to who is taking them. To make sure that she has not missed anything important, Nicole checks her notes against her friends' notes, just to be sure. She also makes index cards from these notes; she says that rewriting the information helps her remember it.

✓ Priority registration; it can be difficult to arrange Nicole's schedule of classes around her athletic commitments.

✓ Accessing the college's tutoring resources. Nicole thinks it is very important to be proactive and seek help before she gets overwhelmed, something her classmates without disabilities do not seem to do.

✓ Study skills and test-taking skills. If professors give out study guides listing the topics students are expected to know for tests, Nicole fills them out. She also studies with friends, which benefits all of them. When she sits down for an exam, Nicole highlights or underlines the questions to make sure that she understands what is being asked and knows what has to be included in her answer in order for her to receive credit. She also highlights her texts.

✓ Talking to professors on an individual basis to explain how her disability affects her functioning. Nicole's professors have been willing and eager to help, she reports, and are open to her requests. (In fact, when she explained to her Sociology professor that it would help her to have copies of the slides she posted before class, the professor decided to post them early for everyone.) Nicole encourages students to visit their professors during office hours, and to remember that professors are there to help: "This is why they are teachers," she says.

✓ Maintaining good study habits. Nicole cautions students not to leave their studying or papers for the night or two nights before an exam or a due date. As she notes, the expectations at college are different from those at high school, and much more studying is required.

Jerome

Jerome is a college graduate with ADD, dyslexia, and an auditory processing disorder. More than a decade older than all the other students interviewed, he grew up during a time when learning disabilities were not well understood, so he did not have the preparation for college that other students with disabilities enjoy. Jerome was not diagnosed until an astute Spanish professor at college suggested that he get tested. After he got diagnosed and applied for services, his accommodations included testing in an isolated room and waivers for science and certain math classes.

Jerome knew something was wrong as early as the second grade, when he could not grasp abstract concepts that offered no relationship that he could internalize, which happened in math and science classes. Jerome reports that he did a lot of cheating starting in third grade and going all the way through high school. Although he's not proud of this technique, he did develop his "people skills" to get students who appeared to "get it" to help him —and these skills have served him well throughout his life. Jerome notes that his parents, who did not know that he had a learning disability, held to the philosophy that "if you didn't get great grades it was because you didn't work hard enough." Even so, they also always emphasized that he "was indeed going to college and would graduate," despite his lackluster school performance.

Jerome's high school grades were not stellar. However, his guidance counselor told him that he "had a gifted intelligence level" and that he "shouldn't worry about all the high school academics" because they would not apply once he got to college.

His counselor's belief in his abilities gave Jerome the confidence to pursue college, where he knew he could be successful. He says:

> High school was horrible on the academic front, but I knew when I got to college that it was where I was meant to be and could flourish intellectually. So, for me, it was just knowing that no matter how bad it got that there was a light at the end of the tunnel.

Having that sense of hope helped Jerome to persevere at school. The knowledge of his disabilities, he says, "revolutionized" Jerome's entire life.

Although some of the interviewees felt it was important to advise students about the more challenging aspects of transition to college, Jerome wants to make sure that they also see the positive aspects:

> College is a much more conducive environment for people with learning disabilities to excel. High school is about memorization. College is about forming and defending a perspective. So, learning is not strictly about what other people think, but what you think about other people. For me, this gave me a context that allowed me to get involved with the work itself. You could internalize it.

Jerome also offers his own cautionary tale. It is not unusual for students with ADD (especially those who do not know that they have it) to be in danger of using alcohol or illegal drugs because they are impulsive or because they are self-medicating. When he was younger, Jerome was "highly susceptible" to these pressures and felt unable to resist these temptations. "The thrill of meeting new friends, being able to take drugs freely, exploring the new learning environment—it was sensory overload and in hindsight I missed out on a lot." He thinks that, if he had known about his ADD before college, such self-knowledge would have made it easier for him to manage his time and himself.

What Worked for Jerome?

✓ Individualized strategies. At the beginning of class, Jerome wrote "LISTEN" on the top of the open page of his notebook; this helped him focus when his attention drifted during class. He performed mental checks, asking himself, "Are you paying attention?" "Are you listening?" "Are you getting anything out of what you are reading?" He even stuck his fingers in his ears when he read to block out distractions.

✓ Socializing with other students who have similar learning problems. Jerome found it helpful to share his issues with people experiencing the same struggles and challenges.

✓ Taking advantage of the college's free counseling; the opportunity to talk freely about his struggles helped sustain Jerome through his difficulties.

Summary

It is interesting that, although all of these students use or used accommodations, they were minimal. Instead of having numerous academic adjustments, these students found techniques that worked for them to keep up with notes and class content. Their experiences echo the themes of the research discussed in Step 1. This should reassure students that, if they work hard and figure out what strategies work best for them, they can find success at college without needing numerous supports.

References

ADA Amendments Act of 2008, P. L. 110-325, 122 Stat. 3553, to be codified at 42 U.S.C. § 12101 (2009).

American Psychiatric Association. (2000). *Diagnostic and statistical manual of mental disorders, fourth edition.* New York, NY: Author.

Banerjee, M. (2009). Technology trends and transition for students with disabilities. In S. F. Shaw, J. W. Madaus, & L. L. Dukes (Eds.), *Preparing students with disabilities for college success: A practical guide to transition planning* (pp. 229–255). Baltimore, MD: Brookes.

Banerjee, M., & Brinckerhoff, L. C. (2009). Helping students with disabilities navigate the college admissions process. In S. F. Shaw, J. W. Madaus, & L. L. Dukes (Eds.), *Preparing students with disabilities for college success: A practical guide to transition planning* (pp. 115–136). Baltimore, MD: Brookes.

Barnard-Brak, L., Lechtenberger, D., & Lan, W. Y. (2010). Accommodation strategies of college students with disabilities. *The Qualitative Report, 15,* 411–429.

Battle, D. E. (2004, February 4). Project Success: Assuring college students with disabilities a quality higher education. *The ASHA Leader.* Retrieved from http://www.asha.org/Publications/leader/2004/040203/f040203b.htm

Brinckerhoff, L. C. (1996). Making the transition to higher education: Opportunities for student empowerment. *Journal of Learning Disabilities, 29,* 118–136. doi:10.1177/002221949602900202

Brown, J. I., Fischco, V., & Hanna, G. S. (1993). *Nelson-Denny reading test.* Rolling Meadows, IL: Riverside.

Dukes, L. L., III. (2009). Gathering data to determine eligibility for services and accommodations. In S. F. Shaw, J. W. Madaus, & L. L. Dukes (Eds.), *Preparing students with disabilities for college success: A practical guide to transition planning* (pp. 167–203). Baltimore, MD: Brookes.

Durlak, C., Rose, E., & Bursuck, W. (1994). Preparing high school students with learning disabilities for the transition to postsecondary education: Teaching the skills of self-determination. *Journal of Learning Disabilities, 27,* 51–59. doi:10.1177/002221949402700108

Elksnin, N., & Elksnin, L. K. (2009). The college search. In S. Shaw, J. Madaus, & L. Dukes (Eds.), *Preparing students with disabilities for college success: A practical guide to transition planning* (pp. 203–228). Baltimore, MD: Brookes.

Faggella-Luby, M., Flannery, K. B., & Simonsen, B. (2009). Using a schoolwide model to foster successful transition to college: Providing comprehensive academic and behavioral supports to all learners. In S. F. Shaw, J. W. Madaus, & L. L. Dukes (Eds.), *Preparing students with disabilities for college success: A practical guide to transition planning* (pp. 83–114). Baltimore, MD: Brookes.

Family Educational Rights and Privacy Act of 1974, 20 U.S.C. 1221 *et seq.* (2008).

Field, S., & Hoffman, A. (2007). Self-determination in secondary transition assessment. *Assessment for Effective Intervention, 32,* 181–190. doi:10.1177/153450 84070320030601

Foley, N. E. (2006). Preparing for college: Improving the odds for students with learning disabilities. *College Student Journal, 40,* 641–645.

Fuchs, D., & Fuchs, L. S. (2006). Introduction to response to intervention: What, why, and how valid is it? *Reading Research Quarterly, 41,* 92–99. doi:10.1598/ RRQ.41.1.4

Getzel, E. E., & Thoma, C. A. (2008). Experiences of college students with disabilities and the importance of self-determination in higher education settings. *Career Development for Exceptional Individuals, 31,* 77–84. doi:10.1177/0885728808317658

Guckenberger v. Boston University, 974 F. Supp. 106 (D. Mass. 1997).

Hadley, W. M. (2006). L.D. students' access to higher education: Self-advocacy and support. *Journal of Developmental Education, 30,* 10–16.

Hong, B. S., Ivy, W. F. Gonzalez, H. R., & Ehrensberger, W. (2007). Preparing students for postsecondary education. *TEACHING Exceptional Children, 40*(1), 32–38.

Individuals With Disabilities Education Act, 20 U.S.C. § 4301 *et seq.* (2006).

Jakubowski v. The Christ Hospital, No. 1:08-CV-00141 (S.D. Ohio 2009).

Janiga, S. J., & Costenbader, V. (2002). The transition from high school to post-secondary education for students with learning disabilities: A survey of college service coordinators. *Journal of Learning Disabilities, 35.* 462–468. doi:10.1177 /00222194020350050601

Jarrow, J. (n.d.). *An open letter to parents of students with disabilities about to enter college.* Retrieved from http://www.ahead.org/affiliates/kentucky/letter_to_parents

Kochhar-Bryant, C., Bassett, D. S., & Webb, K. W. (2009). *Transition to postsecondary education for students with disabilities.* Thousand Oaks, CA: Corwin and Council for Exceptional Children.

Kochhar-Bryant, C. A. (2009). How secondary personnel can work with families to foster effective transition planning. In S. F. Shaw, J. W. Madaus, & L. L. Dukes (Eds.), *Preparing students with disabilities for college success: A practical guide to transition planning* (pp. 137–166). Baltimore, MD: Brookes.

Kravets, M., & Wax, I. F. (2010). *The K&W guide to colleges for students with learning disabilities or attention deficient/hyperactivity disorder (ADHD;* 10th ed.). New York, NY: Random House.

Legal Roundup. (2007). Failure to follow procedures results in lack of disability services, *Disability Compliance for Higher Education, 13*(3), 12.

Legal Roundup. (2008a). Student's discovery of LD comes too late. *Disability Compliance for Higher Education, 13*(12), 14.

Legal Roundup. (2008b). Student must follow college's reasonable procedures to obtain accommodation. *Disability Compliance for Higher Education, 14*(3), 11.

Legal Roundup. (2008c). FERPA authorizes student aides to access education records. *Disability Compliance for Higher Education, 14*(5), 12.

Legal Roundup. (2009a). Denial of academic adjustment results in Title II violation. *Disability Compliance for Higher Education, 14*(7), 12.

Legal Roundup. (2009b). Student can't prove disability discrimination at community college. *Disability Compliance for Higher Education, 14*(8), 11.

Legal Roundup. (2009c). Students' transcripts can't disclose disability status. *Disability Compliance for Higher Education, 14*(8), 12.

Legal Roundup. (2010a). Fee-based disability services violate federal laws. *Disability Compliance for Higher Education, 15*(10), 11.

Legal Roundup. (2010b). OCR faults university for delay in providing accommodations. *Disability Compliance for Higher Education, 16*(2), 12.

Lock, R. H., & Layton, C. A. (2001). Succeeding in postsecondary education through self-advocacy. *TEACHING Exceptional Children, 34*(2), 66–71.

Madaus, J. W. (2003). What high school students with learning disabilities need to know about college foreign language requirements. *TEACHING Exceptional Children, 36*(2), 62–66.

Madaus, J. W. (2005). Navigating the college transiton maze: A guide for students with learning disabilities. *TEACHING Exceptional Children, 37*(3), 32–37.

Madaus, J. W. (2009). Let's be reasonable: Accomodations at the college level. In S. F. Shaw, J. W. Madaus, & L. L. Dukes (Eds.), *Preparing students with disabilities for college success: A practical guide to transition planning* (pp. 10–35). Baltimore, MD: Brookes.

Madaus, J. W., Banerjee, M., & Hamblet, E. C. (2010). Learning disability documentation decision making at the postsecondary level. *Career Development for Exceptional Individuals, 33*, 68–79. doi:10.1177/0885728810368057

Madaus, J. W., & Shaw, S. F. (2004). Section 504: Differences in the regulations for secondary and postsecondary education. *Intervention in School and Clinic, 40*(2), 81–87. doi:10.1177/10534512040400020301

Madaus, J. W., & Shaw, S. F. (2007). Transition assessment. *Assessment for Effective Intervention, 32*, 130–132. doi:10.1177/15345084070320030101

Marshak, L., Van Wieren, T., Ferrell, D. R., Swiss, L., & Dugan, C. (2010). Exploring barriers to college student use of disability services and accommodations. *Journal of Postsecondary Education and Disability, 22*(3), 151–163.

Martin, J. E., Portley, J., & Graham, J. W. (2009). Teaching students with disabilities self-determination skills to equalize access and increase opportunities for postsecondary educational success. In S. F. Shaw, J. W. Madaus, & L. L. Dukes (Eds.), *Preparing students with disabilities for college success: A practical guide to transition planning* (pp. 10–35). Baltimore, MD: Brookes.

Martin, J. E., Van Dycke, J. L., Christensen, W. R., Greene, B. A., Gardner, J. E., & Lovett, D. L. (2006). Increasing student participation in IEP meetings: Establishing the self-directed IEP as an evidenced-based practice. *Exceptional Children, 72*, 229–316.

McGuire, J. (2009). Considerations for the transition to college. In S. F. Shaw, J. W. Madaus, & L. L. Dukes (Eds.), *Preparing students with disabilities for college success: A practical guide to transition planning* (pp. 10–35). Baltimore, MD: Brookes.

Metcalf-Leggette v. Princeton, 3:09-cv-05428 (2009).

Michelle's Law. Pub. L. 110-381, 122 Stat. 4081 (2008).

Milsom, A., & Dietz, L. (2009). Defining college readiness for students with learning disabilities: A Delphi study. *Professional School Counseling, 12*, 315–323. doi:10.5330/PSC.n.2010-12.315

Morningstar, M. E., Frey, B. B., Noonan, P. M., Ng, J., Clavenna-Deane, B., Kellems, R., Williams-Diehm, K. (2010). A preliminary investigation of the relationship of transition preparation and self-determination for students with disabilities in postsecondary educational settings. *Career Development for Exceptional Individuals, 33,* 80–94. doi:10.1177/0885728809356568

National Association of College and University Attorneys. (1997). *Guckenberger v. Boston U.* Retrieved from http://www.nacua.org/documents/Guckenberger_v_BostonU.txt

Newman, L., Wagner, M., Cameto, R., & Knokey, A-M. (2009). *The post-high school outcomes of youth with disabilities up to 4 years after high school: A report from the National Longitudinal Transition Study-2 (NLTS2; NCSER 2009-3017).* Washington, DC: U.S. Department of Education. Retrieved from http://ies.ed.gov/ncser/pdf/20093017.pdf

Peterson's. (2007). *Colleges for students with learning disabilities or AD/HD* (8th ed.). Lawrenceville, NJ: Author.

Prevatt, F., Johnson, L, Allison, K., & Proctor, B. (2005). Perceived usefulness of recommendations given to college students evaluated for learning disability. *Journal of Postsecondary Education and Disability, 18,* 71–79.

Rath, K. A., & Royer, J. M. (2002). The nature and effectiveness of learning disability services for college students. *Educational Psychology Review, 14,* 353–381. doi:10.1023/A:1020694510935

Raue, K., Lewis, L., & Coopersmith, J. (2011). *Students with disabilities at degree-granting postsecondary institutions.* (NCES 2011-018). Washington, DC: U.S. Department of Education, National Center for Education Statistics.

Rehabilitation Act of 1973, as amended by P. L. 110-325, 29 U.S.C. § 701 *et seq.* (2009).

Roid, G. H. (2004). *Stanford-Binet intelligence scales (SB5;* 5th ed.). Rolling Meadows, IL: Riverside.

Section 504 Regulations, 34 C.F.R. § 104 (2009).

Shaw, S. F. (2009). Planning for the transition to college. In S. F. Shaw, J. W. Madaus, & L. L. Dukes (Eds.), *Preparing students with disabilities for college success: A practical guide to transition planning* (pp. 257–283). Baltimore, MD: Brookes.

Simon, J. A., & Lissner, L. S. (2011, May 24). *The ADA as amended: New Title I regulations & determining accommodations: Why should postsecondary education listen to the EEOC?* [AHEAD Audioconference]. http://www.ahead.org/

Sitlington, P. (2003). Postsecondary education: The other transition. *Exceptionality, 11,* 103–113. doi:10.1207/S15327035EX1102_05

Skinner, M. E. (1998). Promoting self-advocacy among college students with learning disabilities. *Intervention in School & Clinic, 33,* 278–284.

Skinner, M. E. (2004). College students with learning disabilities speak out: What it takes to be successful in postsecondary education. *Journal of Postsecondary Education, 17,* 91–104.

Skinner, M. E., & Lindstrom, B. D. (2003). Bridging the gap between high school and college: Strategies for the successful transition of students with learning disabilities. *Preventing School Failure, 47*(3), 132–138. doi:10.1080/10459880309604441

Smith, S. G., English, R., & Vasek, D. (2002). Student and parent involvement in the transition process for college freshmen with learning disabilities. *College Student Journal, 36,* 491–504.

Smitley, B. L. (2000). Factors predicting academic adjustment among college students with learning disabilities. *Dissertation Abstracts International, 61*(10), 3922.

Trammell, J. K. (2003). The impact of academic accommodations on final grades in a postsecondary setting. *Journal of College Reading and Learning, 34*(1), 76–89.

U.S. Department of Education. (2004). *Letter to University of North Alabama re: Disability office records.* Retrieved from http://www2.ed.gov/policy/gen/guid/fpco/ferpa/library/copeuna.html

U.S. Department of Education. (2007). *Transition of students with disabilities to post-secondary education: A guide for high school educators.* Washington, DC: Author. Retrieved from http://www2.ed.gov/about/offices/list/ocr/transitionguide.html

U.S. Department of Education Office for Civil Rights. (2007). *Students with disabilities preparing for postsecondary education: Know your rights and responsibilities.* Washington, DC: Author. Retrieved from http://www2.ed.gov/about/offices/list/ocr/transition.html

U.S. Government Accountability Office. (2009). *Higher education and disability: Education needs a coordinated approach to improve its assistance to schools in supporting students* (GAO-10-33). Washington, DC: Author. Retrieved from http://www.gao.gov/products/GAO-10-33

Webb, K., Patterson, K., Syverud, S., & Seabrooks-Blackmore, J. (2008). Evidenced based practices that promote transition to postsecondary education: Listening to a decade of expert voices. *Exceptionality, 16,* 192–206. doi:10.1080/09362830802412182

Wechsler, D. (2003). *Wechsler intelligence scale for children–fourth edition (WISC-IV).* San Antonio, TX: Pearson.

Wechsler, D. (2008). *Wechsler adult intelligence scale–fourth edition (WAIS-IV).* San Antonio, TX: Pearson.

Wechsler, D. (2009). *Wechsler individual achievement test-third edition (WIAT-III).* San Antonio, TX: Pearson.

Wehmeyer, M. L., & Schalock, R. L. (2001). Self-determination and quality of life: Implications for special education services and supports. *Focus on Exceptional Children, 33*(8), 1–16.

Weinstein, C. E., Schulte, A., & Palmer, D. R. (1987). *The learning and study strategies inventory.* Clearwater, FL: H & H Publishing.

Wilkinson, G. S., & Robertson, G. J. (2006). *Wide range achievement test–fourth edition (WRAT-4).* Lutz, FL: PAR.

Wilson, M. G., Hoffman, A. V., & McLaughlin, M. J. (2009). Preparing youth with disabilities for college: How research can inform transition policy. *Focus on Exceptional Children, 41*(7), 1–10.

Wolinksy, S., & Whelan, A. (1999). Federal law and the accommodation of students with LD: The lawyers' look at the BU decision. *Journal of Learning Disabilities, 32,* 286–291.

Wolman, J. M., Campeau, P. L., DuBois, P. A., Mithaug, D. E., & Stolarski, V. S. (1994). *AIR self-determination scale and user guide.* New York, NY: American Institutes for Research and Columbia University Teachers College. Retrieved from http://www.ou.edu/zarrow/AIR%20User%20Guide.pdf

Woodcock, R. W., McGrew, K. S., & Mather, N. (2001a). *Woodcock-Johnson®. Tests of Achievement III.* Rolling Meadows, IL: Riverside.

Woodcock, R. W., McGrew, K. S., & Mather, N. (2001b). *Woodcock-Johnson® Tests of Cognitive Ability III.* Rolling Meadows, IL: Riverside.

Wynne v. Tufts University School of Medicine, 976 F.2s 791, 932 F.2d 19 (1st Cir. 1992 and 1991, *en banc*).